ESCAPING THE COMING RETIREMENT CRISIS

HOW TO SECURE YOUR FINANCIAL FUTURE

R. THEODORE BENNA
AND WILLIAM PROCTOR

PIÑON PRESS

P.O. Box 35007, Colorado Springs, Colorado 80935

Library of Congress Catalog Card Number: 95-21241
ISBN 08910-99131

Some of the anecdotal illustrations in this book are true to
life and are included with the permission of the persons
involved. All other illustrations are composites of real situations, and any resemblance to people living or dead is coin-
cidental.

This publication is designed to provide accurate and author-
itative information in regard to the subject matter covered.
It is sold with the understanding that the author and the
publisher are not engaged in rendering legal, accounting, or
other professional service. If legal advice or other expert
assistance is required, the services of a competent professional person should be sought. *From a Declaration of
Principles jointly adopted by a Committee of the American
Bar Association and a Committee of Publishers.*

Benna, R. Theodore.
    Escaping the coming retirement crisis : how to
secure your financial future / R. Theodore Benna and
William Proctor.
        p.   cm.
    ISBN 0-89109-913-1
    1. Finance, Personal.   2. Retirement income—
Planning.   3. Financial security.   4. Investments.
I. Proctor, William.   II. Title.
HG179.B395   1995
332.02'01–dc20   95-21241
                                                    CIP

Printed in the United States of America

1 2 3 4 5 6 7 8 9 10 11 12 13 14 15 / 99 98 97 96 95

CONTENTS

—

LIST OF TABLES AND WORKSHEETS

*To our families
and their continuing security in every respect—
personal, financial, and spiritual*

ACKNOWLEDGMENTS

We are deeply grateful to all those who have contributed to the production of this manuscript, including the staff at Piñon Press, our colleagues in our respective offices, and our wives—whose understanding about the necessity of long hours and lost weekends has been decisive in making this book possible.

Thanks Joe Boyle, an actuary from a national retirement planning firm, for generating the tables.

CHAPTER ONE

WILL YOU HAVE ENOUGH MONEY TO RETIRE?

THE GROWING ANXIETY OF AMERICA

A demographic time bomb is ticking. Today, in the mid-1990s, there are nearly five workers for every retiree. In another ten years, by the year 2020, there are expected to be fewer than 3.5 workers for each retiree. And experts are predicting that by 2030, the ratio will be barely *two* workers for every retiree collecting Social Security benefits.

To make up the shortfall in revenues for Social Security, legislators in office at the time of our imagined but all-too-likely neighborhood discussion have had to resort not only to reducing benefits, but also to chipping away at private pension funds through taxes. The situation has created an environment ripe for shattered dreams and bitter generational conflict.

Anxiety is rising today among the general public about whether or not the resources will be available for most people to have a comfortable retirement. In a March 1995 survey conducted by *The New York Times* and CBS News, more than three-fourths of working Americans said that they thought most people their age would face a financial crisis when they retire. Furthermore, 17 percent of the respondents said they were "very worried" that they themselves wouldn't have enough savings for retirement, and 55 percent said they were "somewhat worried" that they wouldn't have enough.

Are these fears rooted in fact? You bet they are.

In the first place, a best-case scenario devised by researchers from Stanford University and Merrill Lynch has revealed that the 76 million baby boomers born between 1946 and 1964 are saving, at the most, 55.6 percent of what they will need to retire comfortably at age sixty-five. Furthermore, a worst-case scenario—with Social Security being reduced and taxes on benefits being raised—shows that these same boomers are saving only 10 percent of what they would need to keep up their current standard of living.

The outlook becomes even gloomier when you consider that most Americans aren't willing to save more, even when they know they will probably be caught short when they try to quit work. Two-thirds of working Americans surveyed by two non-profit groups, the Public Agenda and the Employee Benefits Research Institute, said they knew they could eat out less frequently. But less than a fifth said they would actually take this step to strengthen their retirement preparations (*The Wall Street Journal*, March 24, 1995).

Furthermore, nearly half of those with children under age twenty-two said they felt they could spend less on "extras" for their kids. But only a fifth were willing to cut back on this expense.

Interestingly, this particular study revealed that those with lower incomes—under $25,000 a year—were more willing to save than those with incomes over $40,000. For example, 46 percent of the lower-income people said they could spend less on movies and sports events, but only 29 percent of the higher-income group would take this measure.

Our nation is facing a retirement crisis that is already beginning to cause serious financial hardship for many people, and in the not-too-distant future will trigger significant generational conflict. The emerging scenario is deeply disturbing for the stability and well-being of our society in general—and for your personal future in particular.

Currently, 50 percent of Americans have no employer-provided retirement program at all, and an estimated 90 percent or more will eventually find they have grossly inadequate retirement benefits when they finally try to say goodbye to the working world. In fact, if present trends continue, retirement as we've known it will become a relic of the past for most people.

HOW COULD YOU BE HIT BY THE RETIREMENT CRISIS?

Unless you take charge of your personal retirement planning right now, you will probably be caught in the whipsaw created by the failure of both government and private corporations to live up to their pension promises. In my thirty-five-year career as a retirement planning consultant, and in my role as what *Money* magazine has called the "inventor" of the 401(k) retirement savings plans—which now have an estimated 25 million participants—I've encountered my share of disturbing retirement scenarios. Here is a sampling:

- Now in your mid-thirties, you switched jobs several months ago. You had spent eight years with a company where you were covered by a traditional employer-funded, defined benefit pension plan—the kind that promised to pay you a fixed monthly pension beginning at age sixty-five. But your old company has just advised you that the lump sum value of the pension you earned after eight years' service is a less-than-whopping $1,560. You are astounded to discover how little your employer contributed for your retirement, particularly after they made such a big deal about their "wonderful" pension plan when they hired you.
- You have worked for your company for thirty-five years, and you are ready to retire early, at age fifty-eight—until you discover that such early leisure will reduce the pension you expected to get at age sixty-five by 50 percent, or by 70 percent if you want your spouse to receive a monthly pension after your death.

- You have moved around to several different companies, and with each change, you have improved your career prospects and increased your income—but now, at age fifty-five, you find that the trail of "vested" pension benefits you have accumulated from your various employers will total only a few hundred dollars per month by the time you turn sixty-five.
- You expect Social Security to make up a significant portion of your retirement income at age sixty-five—until you learn that you won't be eligible for full Social Security benefits until at least age sixty-seven, and then you'll lose a considerable part of it to federal income taxes.

The message that these and similar complaints are conveying to us is this: Under current law and business practice, it is highly unlikely that most people will receive the income they need when they retire.

But you don't have to be in this losing category. In the following pages, you'll learn first to identify the specific elements of the crisis that is threatening to deprive you of a comfortable retirement. Then, you'll be provided with a practical, proven program to insure that your later years will be as secure financially as they possibly can be.

What Is Causing the Crisis?

There are several social, political, and economic forces that are pushing us toward a serious financial crunch in our retirement years. It's essential to understand what they are and how they are endangering you if you hope to take effective steps to protect yourself. I'll summarize the major forces briefly at this point, and then we'll go into them in more detail in chapter 2.

Force One: Government interference with the private pension system.

For years the federal government has been passing legislation that discourages employers from establishing or maintaining retirement programs for their employees. Each time the government needs additional revenue, either to fund new programs or to reduce the budget deficit, the private retirement system comes under attack. The reason: it has been identified by government officials as the largest source of lost tax revenue.

In the past, benefits available to individuals through such programs as the Individual Retirement Account have been limited and the imposition of burdensome, red-tape requirements on company plans have prompted some companies to drop those plans. In the future, the interference could escalate to include such measures as taxing some portion of investment income earned on retirement plan assets, or slapping pension principal with a one-time tax. Proposals like this might temporarily increase government revenues—but they would be devastating to your efforts to build a secure retirement income in the future.

Force Two: The disappearance of traditional defined benefit pension plans.

During my years of benefit consulting, I have discovered that corporate benefit decisions are frequently influenced by what is best for senior executives. A decade or so ago, a large portion of the retirement income that senior executives received came from the same pension plans that covered all company employees. Most of these were "defined benefit" plans, which guarantee the worker an annual retirement income based on salary and years of employment, but without any requirement that he or she contribute out of current salary to the pension funds.

When I was recommending benefit improvements fifteen years ago, I found that the top decision-makers were happy to promote the retirement welfare of their employees. After all, they had a very strong self-interest in the impact that any proposed changes in the pension plans would have on them.

Today, the situation is quite different. Benefit and compensation limits have been imposed by the government on defined benefit plans—to the point where the payoff from these plans is a drop in the bucket for the financial security of the nation's senior executives. Also, annual pension expense has become rather unpredictable for most companies. The result may be an unexpected adverse impact on corporate earnings—and top executives and shareholders are never happy when something jeopardizes the company's bottom line.

Because of such factors, companies are likely to continue replacing defined benefit plans with defined contribution plans.

Force Three: The chronic underfunding of some traditional pension plans.

Even if a traditional pension plan stays in place, other dangers may threaten it—including the specter that is known as "underfunding." It's true that *most* defined benefit pension plans are adequately funded. In other words, if they were terminated tomorrow, the assets of the plan would be sufficient to provide the benefits that have been promised. But some plans, such as General Motors, Bethlehem Steel, and Trans World Airlines, have been chronically underfunded. If such a plan were terminated, the assets would be much less than what would be needed to provide the promised benefits.

A federal agency, the Pension Benefit Guaranty Corporation (PBGC), has been established to provide benefits when a terminated plan doesn't have sufficient assets. But if too many companies get into trouble with their defined benefit pension plans during the next ten years, the PBGC could become insolvent. Pension benefits of employees at companies with underfunded plans may then be at risk.

Force Four: The fast deteriorating Social Security system.

Social Security will almost certainly be unrecognizable within twenty-five years—and may be able to play only a minor role in providing for the retirement of Americans, other than those who are close to the poverty line. The current retirement age of sixty-five for full benefits will rise gradually beginning in the year 2000 to a new ceiling of sixty-seven years in 2027. Also, many retirees are *already* paying income tax on much of their Social Security retirement benefits.

But don't expect the restrictions and qualifications to end there. My best advice: Don't count on Social Security *at all* if you are under age fifty—and expect a significant reduction in future benefits if you are over age fifty. At this point, death, taxes, *and* reduced retirement benefits seem virtually certain. Increasing financial pressure to keep the federal bureaucracy afloat will force legislators and other officials to whittle away at Social Security, either by raising the retirement age further, or by reducing benefits.

Force Five: The failure of individuals to properly manage their self-controlled retirement plans. The responsibility for retirement planning is shifting increasingly in *your* direction. We're moving swiftly from employer-funded pension plans, where employees have no responsibility or control, to arrangements where employees have to take active roles.

In future years, the system will become dominated by plans such as the 401(k), 403(b), 457, and IRA—all of which place the burden for retirement planning squarely on the shoulders of the individual. You will have to decide how much to contribute and also how to invest the money in order to accumulate enough to live on comfortably in retirement.

But with this increased freedom comes increased responsibility. Failure to plan properly will mean that you won't be able to retire as you may have hoped. The result may be a substantial reduction in your standard of living during your retirement years. So let the employee who has a self-controlled plan beware—and learn some of the basics of wise investing.

GENERATIONS IN CONFLICT

One of the inevitable results of the economic problems these forces create is potentially bitter social conflict between the older and younger generations. On one side of the battle line, there will be a burgeoning retirement population—estimated to represent about one-third of the total American population in twenty-five to thirty years. These older citizens will demand to receive substantial Social Security benefits because they have spent a lifetime paying their hard-earned money into the program. On the other side, fighting for their own financial survival, will be a severely shrunken group of younger taxpayers who will be faced with an overwhelming economic burden if they have to pay for the retirees' benefits. According to the 1994 Social Security Trustees Report, the payment of Social Security retirement benefits will actually exceed the amount collected in Social Security taxes by the year 2013.

These developments will mean an increase in taxes, or a reduction in retirement benefits, or a combination of the two. In fact, some economic models indicate that the combined employer/employee Social Security tax rate will have to be increased to more than 30 percent of pay to fund these benefits. Such a prospect is unlikely to make the younger generation very happy. The aging of America is one of "the most important demographic developments of the twentieth century," according to The Population Reference Bureau, a private research company.

THERE *IS* HOPE

These trends may seem ominous—and they are. But the outlook is far from hopeless! Beginning right now, regardless of your age or family situation or economic status, you can take decisive steps to make your future considerably more secure. In a nutshell, the approach I recommend is this:

First, assume you are going to retire *tomorrow*. That's right, tomorrow morning you're going to wake up and find your working days are behind you, and an expanse of leisure time extends ahead of you as far as your imagination can reach.

Second, ask yourself this question: "How much money will I need, beginning tomorrow, to live comfortably?" If you are like most people, you will find that 70 to 80 percent of your current salary will enable you to stay at your usual standard of living—mainly because of reduced work-related expenses, such as commuting, new clothes, cleaning, saving for retirement, and the like.

Finally, after you've determined how much you need to retire tomorrow, you will be ready to take some simple steps to project how much money you'll actually need when you quit work. Among other things, you'll have to take into account your desired retirement age and the impact of inflation during the intervening years.

We'll go over the details of all these steps to effective retirement planning in chapters 3 through 7. First, though, let's learn in more detail how to identify and deal with the specific components of the impending crisis that is threatening your financial future.

CHAPTER TWO

WHAT THE CRISIS IS ALL ABOUT

AN IN-DEPTH EXPLANATION
OF WHAT WE'RE UP AGAINST

E ach of the forces I mentioned in the previous chapter poses a peculiar bundle of crises, and all are contributing to a much larger retirement debacle. Let's explore each of these mini-crises in greater depth so that you will be well-informed and well-armed, as you prepare to devise your personal escape route and secure your financial future.

THE FIRST CRISIS: GOVERNMENT INTERFERENCE
IN THE PRIVATE PENSION SYSTEM

As the American fiscal crisis deepens—with increasing concern about the national debt, the federal budget deficit, and the ability of the government to pay for various programs and "entitlements"—legislators and bureaucrats are constantly casting about for fresh sources of revenue. One of the most tempting of these possibilities is the private pension system, with an estimated $4.3 trillion in assets. Some of the proposals to tap these private funds are rather subtle. For example, there has long been talk about forcing the nation's pension managers to make "social investments" in projects that promote the "public good"—as defined by the

21

particular politicians in power. Such a mandate would almost certainly cause pension supervisors to downplay their primary fiduciary duties to get the best return on investments for their participants.

Other recommendations center on the direct taxation of pension funds. Taken together, these trends amount to nothing less than a bald-faced initiative to raid hard-earned money that private companies and individuals have been setting aside for their retirement programs.

To illustrate, here are some disturbing suggestions by leading government officials, several of which were cited in January 1994 by the *Journal of Financial Planning*:

- In a 1992 article in an economic journal, Alicia Munell, who later became Assistant Secretary of the Treasury in the Clinton Administration, made some remarkable proposals: She recommended that existing private retirement funds be assessed a one-time tax of 15 percent. Furthermore, she advocated taxing 10-15 percent of the investment income earned by all the nation's private retirement plans each year. This tax would have been levied against all pensions, from traditional defined benefit plans, to defined contribution programs like the 401(k).
- Both Housing Secretary Henry Cisneros and Transportation Secretary Federico Pena suggested that pension funds should invest in activities that would promote the "social good," such as low-income housing. These views echoed President Clinton's 1992 campaign pledge to build up environmental and transportation systems with pension fund investments.
- Some members of the new Republican Congressional majority have advocated the elimination of all tax deductions—including contributions to private retirement plans—as part of the imposition of a single, flat tax rate.

This is just a taste of the atmosphere that has been developing in Washington. But what anti-pension legislation has actually been passed?

A number of measures have come into law—including an obscure provision in the 1994 General Agreement on Tariffs and Trade (GATT).

The Wall Street Journal raised the alarm in a couple of articles, including a December 5, 1994 report that carried this headline: "GATT Law to Squeeze U.S. Pensions." This piece of legislation also changed the way the maximum contribution limit for 401(k) plans is determined.

The rationale for such changes is that when an employee must cut back on his contributions to such a plan, more of his income becomes taxable. Increasing revenues in this way is supposed to put more money into the depleted federal coffers.

Yet such measures typically backfire. They make it harder for a worker to save, and that, in turn, makes it harder for him to be financially independent when he does finally retire. Obviously, the less independent a person is, the more likely it is that he and his family will eventually require some form of government assistance—and place additional burdens on federal and state welfare programs.

The public was surprised to learn that the GATT measure—which was primarily an international trade bill—contained a provision regulating private pensions and 401(k) plans. Yet this indirect approach to skimming pension funds and self-controlled retirement funds is a tactic that will most likely be used again and again in the future. The reason? It's difficult for politicians to get into our private pension funds with an up-front approach; but it's easy to come through the back door by tacking a pension provision onto an unrelated piece of legislation like GATT.

A more direct approach was tried under the Reagan administration. During the early discussions of the Tax Reform Act of 1986, administration officials proposed eliminating 401(k) plans altogether. Participants in the plans reacted by contacting their Congressional representatives to tell them how unacceptable this proposal was. Such grassroots counterattacks have made government officials wary. Apparently, they now understand that a public announcement that elected representatives are going to go after retirement funds would provoke such a public outcry that their efforts would be stymied.

Every time the government adds extra regulations or makes it harder or less attractive for an employer to administer a retirement program, the company will be more inclined to discontinue the retirement program altogether. The result will be a growing pool of employees who are facing their later years without adequate resources.

Such a result is particularly devastating for smaller employers who don't have a professional staff to cope with such red tape. As a matter of fact, more than 75 percent of the 200,000-plus 401(k) plans cover fewer than fifty employees. Many of these plans are placed at risk each time the government imposes an additional administrative burden, or reduces retirement benefits.

Those of us in the private sector must be extremely vigilant in guarding against the encroachment of government rules and regulations on our hard-earned pension funds—just as our elected officials are protective of their benefits (members of Congress receive pension benefits for every year of their service at a rate that is 70 percent higher than the rate for the highest paid federal civil service retirees). Every cent that the government takes from your investments through taxation or other means is one less cent you'll have for your own comfortable and enjoyable retirement.

THE SECOND CRISIS:
DISAPPEARING ACTS BY DEFINED BENEFIT PLANS

During the early 1980s, several large American companies hired me to help them set up their 401(k) plans, and I suggested it was time to have employees begin saving for their own retirement.

"You don't understand our corporate culture," one executive told me. "We take care of our people for life. They don't have to take charge of their own retirement."

Usually, being "taken care of for life" meant having a defined benefit pension plan, plus liberal, lifetime medical benefits. These programs require no contributions out of employee income and guarantee a stipend for life, depending on the age at retirement and the number of years of service.

This "care-for-life" philosophy had some validity two or three decades ago, but during the past ten years it has changed drastically. Now, increased global competition has forced companies to be much less concerned about employee benefits and much more concerned about the bottom line. We have reached the point where 68 percent of Americans now name "unreliable retirement benefits" as being among the most serious economic problems Americans face, according to a December 1994 *Wall Street Journal*/NBC News poll. Why the dramatic flip-flop in corporate attitudes about defined benefit plans? There are several factors behind the change—and signs are emerging that even more pressure will be placed on companies to get rid of traditional pension systems in the years ahead.

Factor one: First, members of upper management in many large corporations these days have little personal stake in the continuation of traditional defined benefit plans.

In the past, a significant part of a top executive's retirement pay might have come from a defined benefit pension. But today, there is a federally mandated, $150,000 compensation limit for calculating private pension benefits. This means that a CEO of a major corporation, who may earn more than $1 million per year, may be inclined to regard his defined benefit pension payments as little more than a hiccup in his total wealth and retirement package.

Executives at the top earnings levels have a much greater financial stake in stock options and other arrangements than in traditional defined benefit pension plans. In effect, then, two systems have developed in recent years—one for the rank-and-file employees and middle managers, and one for the senior executives.

Of course, there is nothing inherently wrong with giving the highest paid executives lucrative compensation packages. But it's unfortunate that government policy has now separated the fundamental, pocketbook interests of the top executives from those of lower-level employees.

With the financial well-being of high paid senior executives no longer linked to the retirement programs that cover the general work force, we have stepped upon a dangerous, slippery slope. During the next decade, we will almost certainly witness the termination of traditional defined benefit pension plans among many Fortune 1000 companies.

In 1988, for example, Merrill Lynch terminated a pension plan that covered 37,000 employees. The brokerage firm's board of directors subsequently approved a plan that granted Chairman Daniel Tully and his predecessor, William Schreyer, a $1.5 million annual pension for life. If the men died first, their spouses were guaranteed $1.27 million in survivor benefits. You can expect similar moves on the part of other companies in the near future.

For the record, by the way, the median pay—including salary and bonus—for chief executive officers of the large Fortune 1000 companies was an astronomical $1,282,800 in 1993, according to a study by Towers Perrin, the compensation and management consulting firm. Due to the limits imposed by the government, a fifty-year-old executive recruited into a senior position at a major company today will receive a pension benefit from the company's pension plan of only about $25,000 at age sixty-five. But the same executive will typically have the chance to earn millions through stock options, as well as a guaranteed pension of $600,000 or so from a special "top hat" plan covering only senior executives.

The CEO of one big company, who was in this sky-high pay range, was asked about the importance to his retirement of the approximately $100,000 he would receive from his defined benefit pension. His answer: "I suppose every little bit helps."

To understand just how much traditional pensions are being threatened, join me for a moment inside the mind of the typical senior executive in a large company. What motivates him? What makes her tick?

As I've already indicated, the really big payoffs to senior executives today come from stock options—which allow the holder of the option to buy company stock at a price that is typically much lower than the market value of the shares. Obviously, the higher the market value of the stock, the more the options are worth.

So when we read about a CEO receiving $15 million of compensation in a particular year, most of this jackpot typically comes from the exercise of lucrative stock options. But remember, large rewards from stock options require that the price of the company's stock be driven up. So it's in the financial interest of the executive to do everything he or she can to enhance the value of the company's stock.

One way to jack up the stock price is to improve the company's earnings. You see, stock market investors *love* a company that shows increasing earnings (profits) every year. But if you are a senior executive, how, exactly, can you improve your company's earnings? Expenses can be reduced much more quickly than revenues can be raised. So executives are predisposed to take any steps in their power to cut costs—and that often means cutting staff.

In such a corporate environment, if a proposal is put on the table to eliminate a defined benefit program—and increase the value of the stock options of the top executives—there is unlikely to be much resistance. Not all senior executives choose to operate in this "me first" mode, of course, but you can see the incentives the system provides for them to do just that.

Factor two: The second factor that discourages the defined benefit pension system is the negative impact of new government regulations on administering private pension funds.

Various federal rules have introduced considerable unpredictability in calculating pension expenses. For example, one important provision says that pension plan assets cannot exceed by more than 150 percent the current plan liabilities—which are defined as the amount it would cost to pay for all currently earned benefits. This requires a company to determine its pension contribution as if the plan were terminated today, rather than funding the plan's expected future liabilities. This result flies in the face of extensive past experience, which has shown that the most efficient way to meet future pension obligations is to employ a long-term strategy.

Before this funding limit was imposed, employers were able to project with a high degree of accuracy what their current pension contributions should be for them to fulfill future obligations. But now, this is much more difficult, and the projections are less certain to be realized. Because such unpredictability can make corporate profit-and-loss projections a nightmare, a growing number of companies are now reevaluating their defined benefit pension arrangements.

Factor three: A third trend that is endangering defined benefit plans involves a shift that is occurring in the attitudes of human resources managers.

During the next decade, senior human resource positions will be filled by individuals who have grown up in the "defined contribution era." These people, who have been conditioned to prefer defined contribution plans like the 401(k), will oversee most corporate retirement programs. One such human resources executive in her early forties told me, "Defined benefit plans are dinosaurs. They are on the way out. Programs that empower employees to do their own retirement planning are the wave of the future."

While employer-controlled plans may well be a better option, you can see that the perspective held by many of today's human resources executives doesn't bode well for the future of the defined benefit plan.

Factor four: Finally, a fourth factor that is causing defined benefit pensions to play less of a role in American retirement planning is the mobility of our modern work force.

To put it bluntly, even if you join a company that has a defined benefit plan, chances are you will never collect much from it. These plans can pay off handsomely for employees who spend twenty to thirty years working for the same company—*if* they retire no earlier than sixty-five. But defined benefit plans are lousy for mobile, younger employees.

The typical worker these days will change jobs many times during the course of a career—and may even shift careers several times. Consequently, it's becoming increasingly rare to see an employee start with a certain corporation and end up at the same place thirty or forty years later. In fact, there may not be any corporation in existence today that will remain in its present form for the next thirty years!

To better understand the impact that job mobility can have on your pension payout, consider the experiences of two people who enjoyed some success during their active work lives—but were shocked when the time finally arrived for retirement.

HOW DIANE AND JOHN GOT AHEAD—
BUT LOST THEIR PENSION PAY

Diane, who was fifty-nine years old, had changed jobs six times during her career—four times as a result of lucrative offers from other firms, and twice because of a desire to undertake more flexible work when each of her two children was born. The most recent switch had occurred only two years before, when she was fifty-seven.

Every one of the companies Diane worked for provided a defined benefit pension plan, but in every case, she left the job too soon to earn any significant benefits. Twice, she worked for the companies only about four years—too short a time to "vest," or qualify for any of the benefits. The other six times, she worked long enough to vest, but the amount of pay she was entitled to at retirement was minuscule. Even though she was making $55,000 a year, she determined that she would be entitled to only about $6,500 annually from all her private pensions combined when she quit work at age sixty-two.

There were two reasons for her being shortchanged on her retirement pay: First, she had worked only short periods for each company. And second, she had fallen victim to the common rule that when she left a company, her pension benefit was frozen at the *average* salary she had earned during her last five years with the company.

In particular, Diane had failed to understand that in defined benefit pensions, the value of the retirement benefit builds up very slowly in the early years of employment. Benefits rise to their greatest values when the employee is between ages fifty-five and sixty-five.

Suppose that early in your employment history, you work for ten or fifteen years at one certain company, which offers a defined benefit pension, but then you quit at about age forty and make a move to another company. In this case, the lump sum value of your pension from that company is only a small fraction of what the lump sum value would have been if you had worked for that same company, for the same period of time, but at the *end* of your career instead. It's for good reason that these plans are known as "back-end loaded" pensions. See the accompanying graph to get an idea of how these defined benefit pension benefits build up over time.

HOW BENEFITS BUILD UP IN A DEFINED BENEFIT PENSION

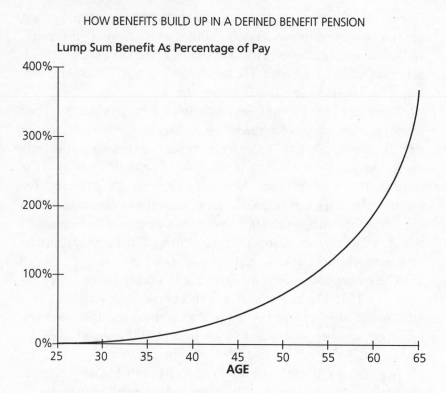

Lump Sum Benefit As Percentage of Pay

A related set of issues confronted John, who worked twenty years for one company with a defined benefit plan. His salary increased to $30,000 per year with this employer, but at age forty-five he accepted an offer from another company for a $5,000 raise. Upon his retirement twenty years later, at age sixty-five, John was earning $55,000.

What kind of retirement did John qualify for? His combined pension from the two companies amounted to only $16,010. If John had stayed with his original company for a total of forty years and retired at age sixty-five with the *same* final salary, he could have received $20,720 per year.

The loss of pension benefits was much less for John than for Diane because he only changed jobs once, and he did not lose time out of the work force. But in fact, *both* of these workers would have been better off with a defined benefit plan.

The following chart contrasts how retirement benefits build with a defined benefit plan versus a comparable defined contribution plan.

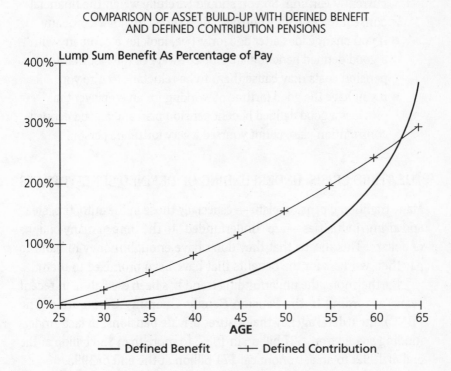

COMPARISON OF ASSET BUILD-UP WITH DEFINED BENEFIT
AND DEFINED CONTRIBUTION PENSIONS

What conclusions should you draw from the experiences of Diane and John? The following are the major lessons to keep in mind:

- Early in your career, look for an employer with a good defined contribution plan, rather than a traditional defined benefit pension plan. Contribute at least 10 percent of your pay, if possible, or whatever your company will match. If you have

already spent fifteen or more years with a company that has a
defined benefit pension plan, where the benefit is based on
your final average pay immediately prior to retirement, the
build-up of your pension benefit will be disrupted if you
change jobs. Your benefit from your current employer will be
frozen at your current average salary, not the salary you're
currently earning. So you should carefully weigh the financial
consequences before considering a move to a new company.

■ If you change jobs after age forty-five, look for a company with
a good defined benefit plan. But be aware of the fact that the
pension costs may cause them to be reluctant to hire you.

■ If you have the good fortune of working for an employer that
provides a good defined benefit pension plan and a good defined
contribution plan, count yourself a very fortunate person!

THE THIRD CRISIS: UNDERFUNDING OF DEFINED BENEFIT PLANS

Many traditional pension plans—especially those in the auto, tire, steel,
and airline industries—are "underfunded" to the tune of many billions
of dollars. This means that they don't have enough money in hand to
pay their workers for the benefits that have been promised to them.

Furthermore, the underfunding trend has been escalating in recent
years, according to the Pension Benefit Guaranty Corporation (the
PBGC), the federal agency that insures private pensions. In fact, underfunding soared from $27 billion in 1987, to more than $53 billion at the
end of 1992, to an astronomical $71 billion at the end of 1993.

Some of the companies with the most seriously underfunded pensions seem curiously unconcerned about this situation. Consider
Ravenswood Aluminum Corporation, which topped the government's
list of corporations with the largest percentage of underfunded pension
plans in February of 1995. The company had $30 million in pension
assets, which were supposed to cover $137 million in liabilities. In other
words, this pension plan was only 22 percent funded! Yet despite its inadequate assets, Ravenswood proceeded to make a deal with its union

workers that called for an *increase* in pension benefits!

Ravenswood Aluminum is not alone. The pension plans in other, much larger companies are also far short of funds. The Pension Benefit Guaranty Corporation reported in 1994 that the companies with the worst record of underfunding included:

- The LTV corporation, with a pension plan that had assets worth only 40 percent of its total liabilities—or in dollar terms, a shortfall of $1.9 billion.
- Tenneco, which was only 46 percent funded, with a shortfall of $227 million.
- The Loews corporation, which was 51 percent funded and had a $153 million shortfall.
- Uniroyal Goodrich Tire, with a plan that was 53 percent funded and assets that fell $450 million short of liabilities.
- Rockwell International, which was 57 percent funded and had a shortfall of $344 million.
- Trans World Airlines, with a pension plan that was 58 percent funded, and a shortage of assets of $426 million.

Fortunately, up to this point the Pension Benefit Guaranty Corporation or the companies themselves have moved to save pension funds that seemed in trouble. For example, in October 1994 the PBGC filed a lawsuit to terminate the severely underfunded pension plan of Western Union, a unit of the New Valley Corporation. The plan was underfunded by $389 million and involved 16,000 employees and retirees.

General Motors, the nation's number one auto maker, acted on its own during 1994 to put an extra $7.7 billion into its pension program. But that still left the fund about $11 billion short of full funding at the end of 1994, though as we go to press, the gap has been reduced to $5 billion.

The underfunding crisis has also crept into the religious community. A study by the William M. Mercer consulting firm reported in November 1994 that the retirement benefits of American nuns, priests, and monks were underfunded by a whopping $6.3 billion! This shortage was so huge that it actually threatened to use up all of the funds of the Roman Catholic religious orders.

But now let's get more personal. What might an underfunded plan in your company—and an inability to meet a shortfall in pension assets—mean to you and your retirement? Obviously, if there are insufficient assets in a pension fund to pay retired workers, the promised benefits will never be paid. In the past, the PBGC has been able to help ailing funds meet their obligations. But many experts worry that if too many corporations—especially large ones, with many retired employees—get into trouble, the PBGC won't be able to cover all the claims.

The agency took over eighty-eight sick plans in 1993, involving a commitment to pay benefits to 346,000 people. With $8.4 billion in assets, the PBGC could meet those obligations—but what might happen if a significant portion of the nation's underfunded plans suddenly went belly-up?

Such a wave of failures would precipitate a pension crisis of earthquake proportions. Even Martin Slate, the agency's executive director, has warned that unless the underfunding issue is addressed soon, the PBGC's "long-term health is in jeopardy" (*The New York Times*, June 11, 1994).

But underfunding isn't the only threat to the federal Guaranty Corporation or the defined benefit system. All employers with defined benefit pension plans are required to pay an annual premium to the PBGC, and the agency is very dependent on this stream of revenue. Uncertainty about the PBGC's financial condition, however, has caused some employers to consider dropping their plans.

During my years of advising employers, this fear of a breakdown of the PBGC was a factor that influenced some of my clients to terminate their plans. And of course, the more companies that terminate their plans, the fewer premium-payers there will be.

How secure is the PBGC's future? When I participated in hearings during one previous effort to shore up the PBGC, the agency offered many assurances that the proposed change would take care of the problem. But another bailout was needed a few years later.

Corporate decision-makers continue to wonder where it will all end—and whether they should trust the government to back up the defined benefit system. As a result, employers with well-funded plans may eliminate the problem by shifting to defined contribution plans.

THE FOURTH CRISIS: THE DECLINE OF SOCIAL SECURITY

Our nation's faith in Social Security these days is weak—and justifiably so. According to a *Wall Street Journal*/NBC News survey released in March 1995, only 14 percent of those polled expected Social Security benefits to pay the same benefits when they retire as it does today. Even more depressing, a hefty 29 percent said they didn't think Social Security would pay any benefits at all.

A majority of older Americans even favor placing some limits on Social Security benefits. According to a *Time Magazine*/CNN poll conducted by Yankelovich Partners in December 1994, 63 percent of Americans aged sixty-five and older agreed that "Social Security recipients who have higher incomes should pay Federal income tax on a larger share of their Social Security payments." Furthermore, 53 percent of these older people said that Social Security recipients with higher incomes should give up some of their benefits.

At the time of this writing, the popular thing for politicians to say is that Social Security is an untouchable "entitlement," which won't be affected by any federal cost cuts or budget-balancing. But there are significant signs of a breaking of ranks on this issue. At least two Democratic members of the House, Representatives Martin Meehan and Joseph P. Kennedy II, have proposed balancing the budget by 2002 by cutting many popular programs, *including* Social Security.

The main reason that some sort of drastic reduction in Social Security benefits seems inevitable is that we are reaching the end of our rope in the funding of the program. The basic truth we have to deal with is that *there is no Social Security fund*, as such. What we have is a phantom trust fund which has nothing in it but I.O.U.s from the government. All benefits are paid out of current revenues. If you are a retiree, and you happen to be sitting next to a younger, working person on some airplane or bus, that "youngster" is actually contributing to the pot that is paying for your benefits.

The danger facing us is three-pronged: First, the proportion of workers who are contributing to the Social Security "fund" out of the FICA taxes, which are deducted from Americans' weekly paychecks, is declining. Second, retirees are living much longer, and so the proportion of retirees who are getting the benefits is increasing. And third, before long, there just won't be enough money coming in to pay out the promised benefits.

Some demographic estimates by the Social Security Board of Trustees and other groups indicate that the ratio of active workers to retirees may be as low as 2:1 by the year 2025—and that simply won't bring in enough money to cover Social Security benefits. In fact, many experts, including the prestigious Committee for Economic Development, believe that the balance between Social Security taxes coming in and benefits going out will shift into the negative column as early as the year 2013. This means that to continue paying benefits at that date, the government will have to find other sources of revenue—and that is *highly* unlikely to happen, given the growing concern about the federal deficit.

The United States is not alone in confronting this crisis. The World Bank has said that the proportion of elderly in the world's population will almost double by 2030, and most governments won't have the resources to support these older non-workers. Italy, Spain, and a number of Latin American countries have already recognized that they are on the verge of their own "social security" crisis—and they are taking steps to put more of a burden on the private sector to take care of retirement pay.

As this worldwide trend gains momentum, it's apparent that even if our own Social Security continues to exist, the system will soon assume a radically different form. Here is what is likely to happen in the near future in the United States:

The Age to Qualify for Full Social Security Benefits Will Rise

Under current legislation, the age for full benefits will increase from sixty-five now to sixty-seven in 2027. So a person born in 1940 will have to wait until age sixty-five and a half, and an individual born in 1950 will be forced to wait until sixty-six. Those born in 1960 won't qualify for full payments until they reach the new top maximum age of sixty-seven.

But don't expect the restrictions to end here. Former Treasury Secretary Lloyd M. Bentsen proposed on NBC's "Meet the Press" that the top age for full benefits be raised to sixty-eight. Former Representatives Tim Penny of Minnesota and Marjorie Margolies-Mezvinsky of Pennsylvania introduced bills that would raise the age for full benefits to seventy by the year 2013. Furthermore, they suggested increasing the age for early retirement from the current sixty-two years to sixty-seven years.

Given current trends, it seems inevitable that the age to receive Social Security benefits will rise—and that means if you want to retire by age sixty-five, you will have to count on other sources of retirement income.

Taxes on Social Security Benefits Will Be Increased

In recent years, retirees have lost increasing amounts of their Social Security, mainly through two types of "tax attacks." The first of these has involved taxing benefits of recipients who are under age seventy and who work. If you are younger than sixty-five when you retire, you have to give up one dollar in benefits for every two dollars you earn over a certain amount. This threshold amount, which is indexed annually at the inflation rate, was $8,160 in 1995. Those retirees aged sixty-five through sixty-nine lose one dollar in benefits for every three dollars they earn over $11,280 (according to indexing in 1995).

Another strategy is to tax the benefits on *all* Social Security recipients whose "adjusted income" exceeds certain levels. In this context, "adjusted income" means the sum of adjusted gross income (as calculated for tax purposes), tax-free interest, one-half of Social Security benefits, and certain income from foreign sources.

Up to 1994, 50 percent of Social Security benefits were taxed when their adjusted income exceeded $32,000 for couples and $25,000 for single taxpayers. After 1994, the government continued to levy that tax, but also added another: Now, up to 85 percent of the benefits are taxed for retirees whose adjusted income exceeds $44,000 for couples and $34,000 for single people.

You can expect two kinds of tax strategies to intensify in the immediate future. "Means testing" will be instituted—so that only retirees with lower incomes will qualify for Social Security payments. In the last months of 1994, a federal advisory panel known as the Bipartisan Commission on Entitlement and Tax Reform submitted some proposals that could be a harbinger of the future for Social Security. The panel—which was headed by Senators Bob Kerrey, a Democrat from Nebraska, and John C. Danforth, a Republican from Missouri—recommended that Social Security payments be reduced for those with wages in the middle and upper income ranges.

What does this mean in practical terms? It means that some sort of legislation will be passed to severely restrict or eliminate Social Security benefits for those with higher incomes. Within the next decade, I believe it is likely that a person whose annual retirement income is in the $40,000 to $50,000 range will receive more limited Social Security benefits. And those in the higher retirement income ranges—say $80,000 or above—probably won't get any Social Security at all.

Social Security (FICA) Taxes on Non-Retired Workers' Income Will Increase

One of the clearest trends during the last two decades has been the increase in Social Security taxes on the wages of active workers. These levies—known as "FICA" taxes, an acronym that stands for "Federal Insurance Contributions Act"—went up from 5.85 percent of wages in 1977 to 7.65 percent in 1990. The maximum taxable wage base increased from $16,500 to $61,200 during this period. As a result, the maximum tax payable jumped from $965 to $4682, a 485 percent increase during an eighteen year period.

The FICA taxes are now applied on income up to a ceiling of $61,200 per year—but that taxable income level has been going up steadily, just like the taxes themselves. All income probably will be taxed at some point in the future. The FICA tax hit is even tougher on small business owners because the law requires that the employer pay Social Security taxes in an amount equal to what the employee pays. These small companies must cough up *another* 7.65 percent, for a total of 15.3 percent on their wages! The rate for the self-employed is 12.4 percent.

As long as the ratio of active workers to retirees continues to decrease, this tax level isn't the end of the story. Unless some unforeseen event causes a cap to be placed on the FICA assessment, you can expect to pay more, possibly as much as 20 percent of your wages (10 percent from the employee, 10 percent from the employer) within the next fifteen years. The percentage could continue to climb up to as high as 30 percent of your wages later.

THE FIFTH CRISIS:
POOR MANAGEMENT OF SELF-CONTROLLED RETIREMENT PLANS

As workers are increasingly forced to rely on their own wits and resources to prepare for their retirement, they are finding that their only viable option is to put their money into "self-controlled" retirement funds. These include the 401(k) for employees of for-profit employers, the 403(b) for employees of most non-profit employers, the 457 for certain governmental employees, SAR-SEP for employees of small for-profit employers, and the Individual Retirement.Account (or IRA). All of these plans require employee contributions, and all except 457 plans may include employer contributions.

This movement of retirement funds into self-controlled plans is booming to the point that there are now more defined contribution plans than traditional, defined benefit pensions. A survey by Sanford C. Bernstein & Company revealed that in 1994 more than 40 million Americans had a retirement plan that required employee contributions. In contrast, 36.5 million American workers were involved in traditional defined benefit plans. The balance tipped in favor of defined contribution plans in 1990 and the trend away from defined benefit plans and toward self-controlled plans has continued ever since.

While this trend can be highly advantageous to the worker who recognizes his or her vulnerability in our current retirement scenario, placing more power into the hands of workers has introduced a whole new set of burdens on our retirement system—burdens that *you* must take into account as you do your own retirement planning. If you don't understand these difficulties and learn how to handle them, you'll eventually find yourself confronting your own personal retirement crisis, with too little income to provide for your needs.

Chances are, you have a self-controlled plan now, or if you don't, you soon will. In other words, you may now be working for a firm that offers *only* a 401(k) or some other contributory plan where you must decide how much to put in and how to invest the money. Or even if you have a traditional defined benefit plan, you may have realized it's necessary for you to begin your own additional retirement fund, such as an IRA, to provide for an adequate retirement.

As you proceed to manage your own retirement planning, here are some of the problems you are certain to encounter—and some suggestions about steps you can take to protect yourself.

Problem One: Failing to Put Money into the Program

This may sound too obvious to mention, but many employees never get to first base with their contributory savings programs because they fail to contribute! You must take the initiative: You have to contribute *first* to trigger a matching contribution by your employer. If you don't take the lead in putting money in, nothing at all will go in.

Here are several suggestions, some of which come from the Financial Literacy Center of Kalamazoo, Michigan, to help you free up money for your defined contribution plan:

- Review your income and expenses for the past six months to one year. Try to identify expenses you might be able to reduce.
- Track your income and expenses for the next month or two. Again, try to identify those expenses you could cut.
- After you've pinpointed the expenses you want to cut, take shopping lists when you go out to buy something—and stick to them. Eliminate impulse spending from your life. Resist

buying anything major unless you've had at least one evening
to sleep on it or talk it over with someone.

■ Find ways that you can save on your taxes—such as by
deducting "hidden" business expenses that your company
hasn't reimbursed you for, or out-of-pocket expenses you've
incurred while doing charitable work. A half hour with a knowl-
edgeable accountant could provide other tax-saving ideas.

■ When you're ready to start accumulating money for long-
term savings, see how much you can reasonably set aside
every month from the expenses and taxes you've saved. Your
goal should be to invest at least 10 percent of your gross
(before tax) income. If you can't manage that, try to save 10
percent of your take-home pay. Remember, if possible you
should increase the percentage you save each time you
receive a salary increase.[1]

■ Pay yourself first. That is, your check to your savings account
should be the first check you write after you get paid every
week. Or even better, have your savings deducted from each
paycheck by your company and deposited directly into your
retirement account. That way, you won't be tempted to delay
your deposit, and you'll be much less likely to regard it as part
of your compensation. Many employees have told me their
defined contribution plan helped them save thousands of dollars they would otherwise have spent. I learned a long time
ago that tithing 10 percent of my gross income to the church
wouldn't work if I contributed to my church what I had left
after paying my bills. Tithing worked only after it became my
first priority. Saving for retirement is similiar—most of us
won't succeed unless it is taken automatically from our pay
each pay period.

■ Always try to find information or techniques that will motivate you to continue saving—as much as you can possibly
manage. I was always inspired to make my contribution when
I recalled that with a plan like the 401(k), I had the

tremendous advantage of being able to invest *pre-tax dollars*. This means that for those in a 33 percent federal and state tax bracket, setting aside $100 a month in a plan will actually reduce take-home pay by only $67. The investor saves the difference of $33 by not paying income tax on the $100 that he has contributed. Remember, you'll never even get started on a self-controlled personal retirement fund if you can't find some way to make those contributions.

Problem Two: Inconsistent Contributions

In too many cases, investors wait too long to start saving for retirement—or they quit making their contributions too soon. Either mistake can end up being disastrous, as you can see from the accompanying chart on page 43.

In the following example, I've assumed that each of the investors has thirty years in which he or she can make annual contributions to a retirement fund, such as a 401(k) or an IRA. But each chose a different approach—with dramatically different results.

Susan waited eight years and then started saving at the rate of $1,250 every year for the next twenty-two years. Specifically, she put in $1000, and her employer matched that with $250. Her total investment was $27,500, and the total value of her accumulated investment, at an 8 percent rate of return, was $71,827.

Unlike Susan, Mark started saving early, in the first year of the thirty-year period, but then he stopped after the eighth year. His total investment was only $10,000, but he ended up with $74,897, or more than Susan—even though he had contributed a total of fourteen fewer years than she did.

Why the big difference? It's simple: Mark put his money in at the beginning of the thirty-year period, and so it had much longer to build up through the power of compounding. That's why I emphasize and *over*emphasize the importance of *putting in your money as early as you can!* If you wait too long, you lose the power of compounding your investment.

Now, take a look at Brian's approach. He started early, and he *continued* to put in his $1,250 faithfully every single year throughout the thirty-year period. As a result, he invested a total of $37,500—only $10,000 more than Susan—but he ended up with a total nest egg of $146,724. That amounts to $74,897 more than Susan's fund, and $71,827 more than Mark's.

What important lesson can we learn from the experience of these three investors? Again, it's rather simple: Begin early, and keep at it! Or even better, start early and *increase* the amount you contribute each year.

WHAT HAPPENS WHEN YOU:
- WAIT TO SAVE
- START EARLY BUT QUIT
- START EARLY—AND KEEP AT IT!

Year	SUSAN waits 8 years to start saving		MARK starts saving early but quits after 8 years		BRIAN starts saving early and keeps at it	
	Annual Investment	Year-End Value at 8%	Annual Investment	Year-End Value at 8%	Annual Investment	Year-End Value at 8%
1	$ 0	$ 0	$ 1,250	$ 1,295	$ 1,250	$ 1,295
2	0	0	1,250	2,695	1,250	2,695
3	0	0	1,250	4,205	1,250	4,205
4	0	0	1,250	5,836	1,250	5,836
5	0	0	1,250	7,598	1,250	7,598
6	0	0	1,250	9,501	1,250	9,501
7	0	0	1,250	11,557	1,250	11,557
8	0	0	1,250	13,777	1,250	13,777
9	1,250	1,295	0	14,879	1,250	16,174
10	1,250	2,694	0	16,069	1,250	18,763
15	1,250	11,557	0	23,611	1,250	35,167
20	1,250	24,579	0	34,692	1,250	59,271
25	1,250	43,713	0	50,973	1,250	94,687
30	1,250	71,827	0	74,897	1,250	146,724
	$27,500 Total Invested	$71,827 Total Value	$10,000 Total Invested	$74,897 Total Value	$37,500 Total Invested	$146,724 Total Value

Problem Three: Early Withdrawal of Retirement Funds

Whatever you do, don't withdraw your money from your 401(k), IRA, or other qualified retirement account before you turn fifty-nine and a half! If you do, you'll most likely have to pay regular income taxes on the distribution, *and* you'll be forced to pay a 10 percent early withdrawal penalty on the principal.

There are a few exceptions to this rule. For example, under some circumstances, you can set up a special early distribution arrangement approved by the IRS. Or if you're disabled, you may be able to start withdrawing the money without penalty. But in general, you have to leave the money in a separate, approved account until you're fifty-nine and a half—or suffer some pretty severe consequences.

If you abide by this "don't-withdraw-early" rule, you'll find there are some major advantages to starting and continuing a defined contribution plan. Suppose you go to work for a company with a 401(k) plan, and then a few years later, you decide to take another job. You are in good shape in this situation because, unlike a traditional defined benefit program, you can take your retirement account with you. In other words, your benefit is "portable"—and you're not penalized for failing to work less than twenty or thirty years at the same company.

So what should you do to protect the retirement money you get from your old company? One option is to put it into a 401(k) plan in your new company. In fact, about 75 percent of all 401(k) plans allow money to be transferred from other 401(k) plans. If you can, arrange to have the old 401(k) money sent *directly* to the new plan so that you don't have a chance to touch it. That will make it clear to the I.R.S. that you have not diverted the funds in any way.

Another possibility is to put your 401(k) money into an IRA through what is known as a "rollover" transaction. But if you choose this rollover option, be sure that you don't mix other funds in the IRA. Otherwise, even if the opportunity should arise later, you won't be able to put the money into another 401(k) plan.

There are some good reasons to be extremely careful in how you handle your 401(k) distribution before you reach retirement age. If you take your 401(k) directly in the form of a check to yourself, you *must* invest the money within sixty days into the second plan, or you'll be hit with income taxes and the 10 percent penalty on your principal. Your employer now is required to deduct 20 percent for taxes if you receive the money directly.

You may have to wait for as long as eighteen months before you are able to join your new employer's plan. If you change jobs six times during your career, you will lose eight to ten years of contributions. So it's essential that you continue to contribute money into a fund for your retirement during these years.

You might use an IRA for this purpose. Otherwise, invest in a mutual fund or other investment on your own. If you fail to take this step, you'll end up with a tremendous retirement fund shortfall. It's also risky to lose the savings habit. Getting used to having the additional money in your pocket will make it more difficult to get back on a more frugal savings track when you become eligible to join another defined contribution plan.

Problem Four: Poor Choice of Investments

Other people get into trouble with a self-controlled plan because they make unwise choices in investing their money. Surprisingly, one of the biggest dangers is being too "safe" or conservative with investments. Although we will go into more detail about the "rules of reasonable risk" later in this book, I want to make a basic point right now about the investment vehicles you should choose for your plan.

Ibbotson Associates, Chicago have determined that between 1926 and 1993, investors could expect the following average annual returns on certain types of investments. These returns include all sources of returns, including interest, dividends, and appreciation of the underlying principal (where applicable).

- For short-term, fixed income investments, such as money market funds or bank certificates of deposit: a 3.7 percent average annual return.

- For bonds and some other long-term fixed income investments: 5.0 percent.
- For "balanced" growth portfolios, consisting of 60 percent stocks and 40 percent bonds: 8.6 percent.
- For "growth" investments, with 100 percent invested in common stocks: 10.3 percent.

There are dramatic variations in the retirement nest egg that you can build up, depending on which of the above strategies you choose. Suppose, for example, that you manage to get $20,000 into your IRA or 401(k) by the time you are forty years old. If you pick the most conservative approach, at 3.7 percent annually—and you don't make any other contributions to the program—you'll end up with $49,602 at the end of twenty-five years.

On the other hand, if you decide to employ the "balanced" portfolio, which has averaged an 8.6 percent return annually, you could expect to have more than three times as much at the end of the twenty-five-year period—or $157,317.

And if you pick the "growth" approach, with solid, blue-chip stocks, historical analysis shows that you will probably earn an average of 10.3 percent per year. That will give you a total principal of $231,962 at the end of the twenty-five years.

Obviously, none of these rates of return is guaranteed. But they do represent the average returns for each of these investment strategies during the period 1929–1993. Furthermore, the chances are that you can match them if you employ a wise, disciplined approach to investing.

One thing is absolutely certain, however: If you pick the "safest" approach, with the lowest rate of return, you won't be safe at all. Instead, you'll end up with a relatively small nest egg that won't give you the income you need for a truly comfortable retirement.

Problem Five: Poor Management of the Program
Organizations such as mutual fund companies that invest retirement money for 401(k)s and IRAs are forced to compete to attract and retain

investors. Because historical investment performance influences most investors, fund managers are under intense pressure to perform.

Consequently, managers sometimes take a higher degree of risk in an attempt to enhance their investment results, and this increased risk may result in financial failure. The failure of several large insurance companies in recent years (including Mutual Benefit and Executive Life Insurance) caused 401(k) participants who had money invested in these plans to receive less than they had expected. Participants in other plans have been hurt by derivative losses—including members of the 457 plan in Orange County in Southern California.

With 401(k) and similar plans, the selection of the organizations that will invest the money is up to the employer. In most cases, you will be given a choice of several investment options. The selection of funds offered is usually handled in a professional manner, particularly in large companies. The plan sponsor is required legally to consider only the options that are in the best interest of the participants. Among other things, all contributions to employee-controlled plans must be transferred to a separate legal entity outside the control of the plan sponsor. This way, if the employer goes out of business, the plan's assets are protected.

Still, there is enough of a danger in this area that several major agencies—including the Securities and Exchange Commission (SEC), the Federal Trade Commission (FTC), and the North American Securities Administrators Association (NASAA)—have issued warnings. In December 1994, these groups reported that fraudulent schemes have robbed workers of hundreds of millions of dollars in funds these had invested in some defined contribution plans.

How can you protect yourself? Federal regulators have suggested several ways, according to reports in *The Wall Street Journal* and elsewhere:

- Avoid investments advertised as "IRA-approved" or "endorsed by the Internal Revenue Service." Such endorsements or approvals don't exist.

- Don't transfer your IRA or other retirement funds directly to an individual. The money should go directly to an institution, such as a bank or a mutual fund company.
- Don't forget that you—not your bank, broker, or other IRA custodian—are responsible for monitoring the condition of your investments.
- Be suspicious of investments that are the subject of a hard sell on a paid TV program or other advertisement.
- Above all, don't allow yourself to be pressured into making quick decisions. Always double- and triple-check an investment company before you make a commitment.

Following these guidelines won't necessarily ensure that you'll find the best investment company or advisor. But at least you'll increase the odds in your favor.

THE RESULT OF THE CRISIS: CONFLICT BETWEEN GENERATIONS

Finally, as I've already discussed in some detail, our retirement system is in serious trouble because of a fundamental social problem we are facing—the coming confrontation between the old and the young in our population.

A steadily declining pool of younger workers is staring at the bleak reality of having to meet the demands of a burgeoning mass of retirees. These retirees—who will find themselves seriously strapped for funds—will look to the government for support, and the active workers will resist being saddled with extra taxes or other financial burdens.

Furthermore, younger people are likely to be blindsided from another, unexpected source—the pressure of increased medical costs and benefits for the elderly. You may be wondering what medical benefits have to do with the security of your retirement income. The answer is *a great deal*—for a number of reasons.

Medical coverage and costs are a major issue for retirees for the obvious reason that as you grow older, your medical needs and costs often increase. If you have to pay for doctor and hospital expenses out of your own pocket, you can quickly find yourself with little left over for other purposes.

Some employers do provide medical coverage for retirees, but I always advise my clients not to count on this benefit continuing indefinitely. One problem is that most major companies agreed to provide retiree medical coverage years ago without understanding the long-term cost. During recent years, those same employers have been scrambling to reduce this expense because retiree medical costs have escalated dramatically. Also, medical expenses typically have to be paid from current company revenues. Consequently, they threaten the company's bottom line and profits—unless the company passes on its costs to the consumer in the form of higher prices. For example, the auto industry has reported that $1,000 of the price of each car is used to cover health care costs. And a large portion of this expense goes for retiree medical benefits.

But Isn't Medicare a Safety Net?

An even more fundamental problem is that most retirees rely not on a company plan, but on Medicare as the primary source of their medical coverage. In fact, many people I know blithely assume that all their medical needs will be covered forever by the federal government after they turn sixty-five.

But there are storm clouds that loom over this rosy horizon—clouds that could result in a devastating hit on your retirement funds. First of all, Medicare coverage is available only for those who are age sixty-five or older. As a result, access to affordable medical coverage can become a major concern for any retiree who is *under* age sixty-five, or who has a dependent under sixty-five. So if your spouse or anyone else in your family will be younger than sixty-five at your retirement, you have to plan to pay for medical coverage for these people out of some source other than Medicare.

Another concern is the status of the basic funding for the Medicare program. Medicare is in effect a pay-as-you-go system. Taxes collected during a given budget year are used to pay for current benefits. The system has virtually no reserves—and that means when government revenues are tight, Medicare payments may be threatened.

It was mostly the realization that the Medicare system was in serious financial trouble that prompted President Clinton to attempt to overhaul the entire national health care system in 1994. That initial attempt failed, but Republican budget-balancers have been open about targeting Medicare for cost-cutting. So some sort of revamping of the Medicare and medical insurance still seems inevitable.

As our population ages and the costs of medical care continue to rise, something must give—and soon. Even now, the most rapidly growing segment of our population is the over-eighty-five crowd, and we can expect the demographic balance to continue to shift more and more toward the older generation. As this happens, the older citizens will become more vocal in demanding good health care, the younger people will balk at paying for it, and the ensuing fight will exacerbate further the conflict between the generations. It could get extremely ugly—but for you, there is an escape route.

Reflect for a moment on the various crises we've been exploring in this chapter—such as the problems with traditional defined benefit plans, the weakening of Social Security, and the failure of workers to plan effectively on their own. These are laying a solid and discouraging foundation for the impending retirement crisis. But you can avoid the dilemmas we've talked about—if you take the steps outlined in the following chapters. Get a pencil and let's get started on your strategy for securing your financial future.

NOTE

1. You may not be able to contribute 10 percent of your income to your defined contribution plan because your plan doesn't allow that large a contribution. In such a case, you should put as much as you can into your company plan. Then, invest the rest in another plan, such as an IRA or even an "unqualified" personal investment account that isn't linked to any federal retirement plan. The important thing is to free and invest as much money as you possibly can to prepare for your retirement.

CHAPTER THREE

BEGIN YOUR ESCAPE—BY RETIRING TOMORROW

HOW MUCH MONEY WOULD YOU NEED?

The time has now arrived for you to determine how much money you will need and where you'll get it in order to retire safely and comfortably—but we're going to take a rather unusual, "back-door" approach to this issue. No matter how old you are now, I first want you to assume that *you are going to retire tomorrow*. Whatever calculations you have to make will all be based on this initial assumption.

Why am I suggesting this approach? First, I've found that it always helps to have a dollar figure in mind at the outset of your planning—even if it becomes necessary to adjust that figure at some point during your calculations. When you are hit between the eyes with a specific income that you need, this dollar-and-cents wake-up call can provide a reality check and motivate you to action. When you can say with conviction, "I know that if I quit work tomorrow, I would need at least . . . to live comfortably," you'll be forced to ask yourself automatically, "How will I get the kind of nest egg I need to produce this level of income when I retire?"

Second, I've found after working for decades with men and women who are trying to prepare for retirement that it's essential to do everything possible to keep your eyes from blurring over with complicated calculations. While planning effectively for retirement always requires

51

some juggling of numbers, even relatively simple calculations can trigger a serious case of "math phobia" in many otherwise well-educated people. But most people can sidestep any inner resistance they may feel—and become thoroughly absorbed in the process of retirement planning—if they can identify *immediately* the minimum amount they would need to retire if they quit work tomorrow.

Third, you need to establish a realistic targeted retirement age. Most employees under age fifty expect to retire between the ages of fifty-five and sixty. As you will see when we get into the scenarios, being financially prepared to retire at age sixty-five will be a major challenge for most of us.

In this chapter, we'll deal with the actual steps you should go through if you are now sixty-five and you plan to quit work this year—even though you may have done little or nothing to prepare for this momentous new adventure in your life. I'm always surprised at the number of people who wait until the last minute to do their retirement planning. Still, even though this kind of procrastination isn't advisable, there are effective measures that can make a last-minute decision to retire an easier experience. And remember, the points we will be discussing in this section will also be helpful to younger people, who are concerned about achieving their long-term financial goals. Even if you are thirty-five or forty-five, you can learn a great deal—and get off to a good start in your own preparations—if you go through the steps outlined in this chapter.

Now, let's move on to the first question that *everyone* should ask at the outset of any retirement planning: How can I determine how much income I would need if I quit work tomorrow?

The best first step for anyone planning for retirement is to start with your current income, then multiply by 70 to 80 percent to determine the amount you'd need to keep your standard of living stable if you retired immediately. Next, identify current assets that could generate the income you need—and if you find you are still short of money, double-check to see how you might be able to generate the needed income from the assets you have.

Let's examine in some detail the planning steps that should be taken by Arnold, who really *is* sixty-five years old, and who is now making $37,500 a year.

HOW TO RETIRE TOMORROW

I will assume for the sake of simplicity that Arnold is single. I would recommend, just to be safe, that he plan to retire on 80 percent of his current income, or $30,000.

Will Arnold be comfortable on this amount of money? Obviously, if he plans to retire in New York City or San Francisco, he may need considerably more. But if he selects a part of the country where expenses are lower than in the big cities or resort areas, $30,000 can be quite adequate for a single person.

So how will Arnold get the money he needs to be able to quit work tomorrow? First, there is Social Security. Under present law, Arnold will be eligible for Social Security benefits of about $12,000 a year.[1] Also, he is entitled to receive $400 a month as a lifetime pension from his company. The defined benefit pension plus the Social Security adds up to $16,800 annually—but that leaves another $13,200 unaccounted for. How much principal would it take to generate that much money—and where might Arnold get it?

The answer to this question depends on several variables:

- The number of years planned for retirement—in other words, how long Arnold expects to live.
- The rate of inflation.
- The investment return expected during the retirement years.
- The amount of principal invested to generate the needed income.

Let's examine each of these variables in more detail and see what kind of an impact they have on Arnold's retirement planning.

The number of years retired. This question could also be asked in a couple of other ways: "How long does Arnold expect to be in retirement before he goes back to work?" Or more likely, "How long does Arnold expect to live?"

It's most reasonable to assume that neither Arnold—nor you— would want to return to work at age seventy-five or eighty, after years away from the workplace. But because it's impossible to predict exactly when death will occur, I recommend using at least age ninety for the end of retirement, rather than the normal life expectancy.

Remember, many people live well beyond the normal average life expectancy—which is determined by statistical projections, rather than by what actually happens to any given individual. As for me, I might like to be surprised by living ten or fifteen years longer than anyone expected. But I *wouldn't* want to be surprised by not having enough money to live comfortably during those extra years—and I'm sure Arnold wouldn't either!

The rate of inflation during retirement. The rate of inflation won't stop when you retire. The cost of living continues to increase—and the increase could be dramatic if the government fails to do a good job of managing its budget, expenditures, and interest rates. Fortunately, in recent years the rate has hovered between 3 and 4 percent a year, and it has averaged 3.1 percent from 1936 through 1993. I will be assuming a 3.5 percent rate in Arnold's case.

What this all means is that after you retire, you will need more money each year than you needed in the previous year if you hope to maintain your standard of living. Here is how Arnold must project for this reality. If he assumes an inflation rate of at least 3.5 percent per year, the extra $13,200 he needs now will have to increase to the following amounts in the future:

RETIREMENT INCOME ARNOLD WILL NEED

Age	Income Needed
65	$13,200
70	$15,708
75	$18,612
80	$22,176
85	$26,268
90	$31,284

In other words, at a 3.5 percent inflation rate, $31,284 will have the same purchasing power twenty-five years from now as $13,200 does today. That is how much money Arnold will have to be bringing in during his ninetieth year—if he wants to maintain his standard of living.

The accompanying table 3-2, which you will see often in later parts of this book, will show you how to figure out what any lump sum today will be worth in a given number of years, at a given rate of inflation, or change. If Arnold assumes a 3 percent rate of inflation for the next twenty-five years instead of a 3.5 percent rate, he would need $27,588 at age ninety—as compared with $13,200 at age sixty-five. (He would just multiply 2.09, the factor next to the year 25 in the chart, by the $13,200 he began with.)[2]

Table 3-2

INFLATION ADJUSTMENT TABLE

Number of Years	Assumed Annual Rate of Change				
	3%	*3.5%*	*4%*	*4.5%*	*5%*
1	1.03	1.035	1.04	1.045	1.05
2	1.06	1.07	1.08	1.09	1.10
3	1.09	1.11	1.12	1.14	1.16
4	1.12	1.15	1.17	1.19	1.22
5	1.16	1.19	1.22	1.25	1.28
6	1.19	1.23	1.27	1.30	1.34
7	1.23	1.27	1.32	1.36	1.41
8	1.27	1.32	1.37	1.42	1.48
9	1.31	1.36	1.42	1.49	1.55
10	1.34	1.41	1.48	1.55	1.63
11	1.38	1.46	1.54	1.62	1.71
12	1.42	1.51	1.60	1.70	1.80
13	1.46	1.56	1.67	1.77	1.89
14	1.51	1.62	1.73	1.85	1.98
15	1.56	1.68	1.80	1.93	2.08
16	1.60	1.74	1.87	2.02	2.18
17	1.65	1.80	1.95	2.11	2.29
18	1.70	1.86	2.02	2.21	2.41
19	1.75	1.93	2.10	2.31	2.53
20	1.80	1.99	2.19	2.41	2.65
21	1.86	2.06	2.28	2.52	2.79
22	1.91	2.13	2.37	2.63	2.93
23	1.97	2.21	2.46	2.75	3.08
24	2.03	2.29	2.56	2.87	3.23
25	2.09	2.37	2.66	3.00	3.39
26	2.15	2.45	2.77	3.14	3.56
27	2.22	2.53	2.88	3.28	3.74
28	2.28	2.62	3.00	3.43	3.92
29	2.35	2.72	3.12	3.58	4.12
30	2.42	2.81	3.24	3.74	4.33

The expected return on investment. Perhaps the most important factor that will influence the size of Arnold's nest egg is his rate of investment return. This refers to the average annual growth he can expect on his principal during his retirement years.

What determines this rate of return? When you are figuring this out for yourself, it all comes down to how much risk—and year-to-year fluctuations or volatility in your investments—that you are willing to assume. The more stable and less volatile your investments, the lower growth in principal that you can expect. And the greater the volatility, the greater the chance for long-term reward.

Now let me warn you: I'm about to make some suggestions that will turn much conventional investment advice on its ear. Older people like Arnold usually shift all or most of their resources into fixed-income investments shortly before or at retirement. Many "experts" have told us that we should be aggressive and invest heavily in stocks when we are young, and then shift to "safe," income-producing investments—such as bank certificates of deposit, Treasury bills, or money market funds— when we grow older.

The logic behind this advice is that we need income at retirement, so we should position our money in investments that produce higher, more immediate income from interest and dividends. Unfortunately, history reveals that such investments provide lower long-term returns than do aggressive stocks, which have lower dividends. Such a strategy may have been reasonable when retirees could expect to live for only ten or twelve years after retiring. But this approach is dangerous these days, when many live much longer.

For example, when my parents first retired about twenty-five years ago, they decided to put all their personal funds into bank certificates of deposit and money market funds. This way, their principal remained completely stable and was protected by federal insurance programs for bank deposits. Also, when they invested in these bank certificates in the early 1980s, they were able to earn double-digit interest for a while. After those rates dropped, they put their funds into bank certificates at 7 to 8 percent a year.

But like many other retirees, they experienced a tremendous drop in their income when interest rates on these instruments dropped down to about 3 to 4 percent in the early 1990s. Furthermore, the purchasing power of their income has become much less than it was twenty-five years ago—because of the increased cost of living. The monthly rent on their three-bedroom home in a central Pennsylvania town has increased from $65 to $250 per month.

Assume, for instance, that they held $100,000 in bank CDs. In the mid to late 1980s, they received approximately $7,000 in interest income on this principal—an amount which, combined with their Social Security benefits and a pension, has allowed them to live quite comfortably. But then the interest income dropped to around $3,000 by the early 1990s, and yearly inflation further reduced the buying power of this income to about $1,500. Imagine having your income drop by 80 percent in the space of just a few years! Fortunately, their Social Security and employer-provided pension have both increased over the years and have helped cushion the impact of inflation.

This conservative strategy is okay if you only live for ten years or so after you retire; however, it is risky if you live for twenty or thirty years. Your purchasing power will be seriously eroded if you do not maintain a significant portion of your assets in investments that have the potential to produce a higher return than the inflation rate.

Three Investment Strategies

Before we return to Arnold's situation, I want to make a few points about some investment strategy categories I've chosen to use here and elsewhere in this book. Basically, there are three investment strategies you can choose from: conservative, moderate, or aggressive. But these are relative terms that may have different meanings at different times in your life.

For those who have years to go before they retire, their strategy should involve higher risks at potentially higher long-term investment returns than for those who are near or at retirement. A retired person should be reasonably aggressive in his investing if he hopes to keep up with the cost of living, while remaining more conservative overall than an active worker who has many years to go before retirement.

I assume in this book that "conservative" investing for a working forty-year-old means an annual return of 6.2 percent—whereas for a retiree, "conservative" means a lower, 5.2 percent return. Similarly, for a forty-year-old, "moderate" involves an 8.6 percent return, while "moderate" for a retiree is 7.4 percent. And "aggressive" for a forty-year-old worker would be 10.3 percent, but "aggressive" for a retiree would be 8.6 percent.[3]

The highest, most aggressive rates for active workers will require more volatile investments, such as growth stocks. But the retiree can probably achieve the higher rates by sticking to a mixture of more stable blue chip stocks, high-quality bonds, and some other fixed-income instruments.

In actual monetary terms, here is how this process works. Assume you need an annual $10,000 income for your retirement, which must be produced from your retirement nest egg—not from Social Security or a company pension. Also, you want the purchasing power of that income to stay steady.

The following charts show how much principal you would need to generate that $10,000 in inflation-adjusted income using the three different investment strategies over a twenty-five-year period.[4] These figures assume a 3.5 percent inflation rate.

Table 3-3

MANAGING YOUR NEST EGG OVER TWENTY-FIVE YEARS
Conservative Investment Strategy—5.2% Return

Number of Years	Beginning of Year Balance	Annual* Withdrawal	Investment Return	End of Year Balance
1	201,910	(10,000)	10,239	202,149
2	202,149	(10,350)	10,243	202,042
3	202,042	(10,712)	10,228	201,558
4	201,558	(11,087)	10,193	200,664
5	200,664	(11,475)	10,136	199,324
6	199,324	(11,877)	10,056	197,503
7	197,503	(12,293)	9,951	195,162
8	195,162	(12,723)	9,818	192,257
9	192,257	(13,168)	9,655	188,744
10	188,744	(13,629)	9,460	184,575
11	184,575	(14,106)	9,231	179,700
12	179,700	(14,600)	8,965	174,065
13	174,065	(15,111)	8,659	167,614
14	167,614	(15,640)	8,309	160,283
15	160,283	(16,187)	7,914	152,010
16	152,010	(16,753)	7,469	142,726
17	142,726	(17,340)	6,971	132,357
18	132,357	(17,947)	6,416	120,826
19	120,826	(18,575)	5,800	108,051
20	108,051	(19,225)	5,119	93,945
21	93,945	(19,898)	4,368	78,415
22	78,415	(20,594)	3,542	61,363
23	61,363	(21,315)	2,637	42,685
24	42,685	(22,061)	1,646	22,270
25	22,270	(22,833)	564	0
TOTALS		(389,499)	187,589	

Equal to $10,000 adjusted annually for inflation assuming a 3.5% inflation rate. It has been assumed the withdrawal will take place at the middle of the year.

Table 3-4

MANAGING YOUR NEST EGG OVER TWENTY-FIVE YEARS
Moderate Investment Strategy—7.4% Return

Number of Years	Beginning of Year Balance	Annual* Withdrawal	Investment Return	End of Year Balance
1	160,430	(10,000)	11,502	161,932
2	161,932	(10,350)	11,600	163,182
3	163,182	(10,712)	11,679	164,149
4	164,149	(11,087)	11,737	164,799
5	164,799	(11,475)	11,771	165,099
6	165,094	(11,877)	11,778	164,996
7	164,995	(12,293)	11,755	164,458
8	164,458	(12,723)	11,699	163,434
9	163,434	(13,168)	11,607	161,873
10	161,873	(13,629)	11,474	159,718
11	159,718	(14,106)	11,297	156,909
12	156,909	(14,600)	11,071	153,380
13	153,380	(15,111)	10,791	149,060
14	149,060	(15,640)	10,452	143,872
15	143,872	(16,187)	10,048	137,733
16	137,733	(16,753)	9,572	130,552
17	130,552	(17,340)	9,019	122,231
18	122,231	(17,947)	8,381	112,665
19	112,665	(18,575)	7,650	101,740
20	101,740	(19,225)	6,818	89,333
21	89,333	(19,898)	5,875	75,310
22	75,310	(20,594)	4,811	59,527
23	59,527	(21,315)	3,616	41,828
24	41,828	(22,061)	2,279	22,046
25	22,046	(22,833)	787	0
TOTALS		(389,499)	229,069	

Equal to $10,000 adjusted annually for inflation assuming a 3.5% inflation rate. It has been asumed the withdrawal will take place at the middle of the year.

Table 3-5

MANAGING YOUR NEST EGG OVER TWENTY-FIVE YEARS
Aggressive Investment Strategy—8.6% Return

Number of Years	Beginning of Year Balance	Annual* Withdrawal	Investment Return	End of Year Balance
1	143,065	(10,000)	11,874	144,939
2	144,939	(10,350)	12,020	146,609
3	146,609	(10,712)	12,148	148,045
4	148,045	(11,087)	12,255	149,213
5	149,213	(11,475)	12,339	150,077
6	150,077	(11,877)	12,396	150,596
7	150,596	(12,293)	12,423	150,726
8	150,726	(12,723)	12,415	150,418
9	150,418	(13,168)	12,370	149,620
10	149,620	(13,629)	12,281	148,272
11	148,272	(14,106)	12,145	146,311
12	146,311	(14,600)	11,955	143,666
13	143,666	(15,111)	11,706	140,261
14	140,261	(15,640)	11,390	136,011
15	136,011	(16,187)	11,001	130,826
16	130,826	(16,753)	10,531	124,604
17	124,604	(17,340)	9,970	117,234
18	117,234	(17,947)	9,310	108,597
19	108,597	(18,575)	8,541	98,563
20	98,563	(19,225)	7,650	86,988
21	86,988	(19,898)	6,625	73,715
22	73,715	(20,594)	5,454	58,575
23	58,575	(21,315)	4,121	41,381
24	41,381	(22,061)	2,610	21,930
25	21,930	(22,833)	904	1
TOTALS		(389,499)	246,434	

Equal to $10,000 adjusted annually for inflation assuming a 3.5% inflation rate. It has been assumed the withdrawal will take place at the middle of the year.

As you can see from these tables, the three different investment strategies present quite different pictures, both in terms of the initial amount of principal required and the amount of income that principal produces over a twenty-five-year period. To generate $10,000 in inflation-adjusted income over this period, a conservative strategy at a 5.2 percent return per year would require you to start out with $201,910. Furthermore, in only the fourth year, your principal amount would be lower than what you began with. To achieve the very same income, a moderate strategy at a 7.4 percent rate of return requires you to put up only $160,430. In this case, your principal would not dip below this starting amount until the tenth year. Finally, with an aggressive strategy, at an 8.6 percent rate of return, you could begin with an investment of only $143,065. Your principal would not move below this start-up investment amount until the thirteenth year.

Some people choose the conservative investment strategy—investing their entire nest egg in bank certificates of deposit, Treasury bills, and bonds with short to intermediate maturities—because it provides the greatest protection from big changes in their underlying principal as a result of unstable markets or financial problems in specific companies. They receive a safe, steady interest income that varies only with swings in interest rates.

But there *are* some risks with the conservative strategy: Inevitably, inflation will chew away at the value of your principal and income. Also, interest rates may drift to very low levels, as they did in the early 1990s. Because you are likely to live for twenty to thirty years after you retire, the purchasing power of your interest income will be eroded as a result of inflation.

To jack up your purchasing power by using the moderate investment strategy, you would need to rearrange your portfolio to include about 40 percent in common stocks, 40 percent in high-grade corporate and government bonds, and 20 percent in cash reserves, such as bank certificates of deposit and money market funds. If you can endure shifts in the market with equanimity and a sense of perspective, and you want to try the aggressive strategy, you would put about 60 percent of your portfolio into common stocks, 40 percent in bonds, and virtually nothing in cash.

In my consulting experience, I have found that most retirees cannot live with the severe ups and downs that often accompany an aggressive portfolio. It may take years of experience to be comfortable operating as an aggressive investor. Experienced investors know that the odds are excellent that the long-term movement of the stock of good companies is going to be up, not down. But even if you can't go all the way and embrace an aggressive strategy, I would strongly urge you not to be satisfied with the conservative approach. The increasing cost of living is almost certain to leave you with seriously eroded principal and much less income than you need to live comfortably. Instead, go for the moderate strategy—and put yourself in a much stronger position to see your income keep up with inflation.

Now that we have explored some of the basic features of the three investment strategies, let's move on to the final element upon which successful retirement planning depends: the amount of principal invested. Exactly how much of a nest egg does Arnold need as he begins his plan to retire tomorrow—and what approach should he take to get it?

The amount of principal invested. How much money will Arnold need to produce his extra $13,200 of income? To figure out the principal he needs, he should use table 3-6, which shows how much is needed to produce one dollar of inflation-adjusted income at the conservative, moderate, or aggressive rates over a twenty, twenty-five, or thirty year period. (All tables in this book are reprinted in the Appendix for easy reference.)

Table 3-6

AMOUNT NEEDED TO PROVIDE ONE DOLLAR
OF INFLATION-ADJUSTED INCOME AFTER RETIREMENT

Inflation Rate—3.0%			
Investment Strategy	**Number of Years Income Will Be Needed**		
	20	**25**	**30**	**35**
Conservative	$16.08	$19.14	$21.90	$24.38
Moderate	13.36	15.29	16.85	18.12
Aggressive	12.16	13.67	14.82	15.71

Inflation Rate—3.5%			
Investment Strategy	**Number of Years Income Will Be Needed**		
	20	**25**	**30**	**35**
Conservative	$16.78	$20.19	$23.33	$26.23
Moderate	13.91	16.04	17.82	19.30
Aggressive	12.64	14.31	15.62	16.65

Inflation Rate—4.0%			
Investment Strategy	**Number of Years Income Will Be Needed**		
	20	**25**	**30**	**35**
Conservative	$17.53	$21.32	$24.90	$28.25
Moderate	14.47	16.85	18.88	20.61
Aggressive	13.13	14.99	16.48	17.69

Inflation Rate—4.5%			
Investment Strategy	**Number of Years Income Will Be Needed**		
	20	**25**	**30**	**35**
Conservative	$18.32	$22.53	$26.60	$30.54
Moderate	15.08	17.72	20.03	22.04
Aggressive	13.66	15.72	17.42	18.82

Inflation Rate—5.0%			
Investment Strategy	**Number of Years Income Will Be Needed**		
	20	**25**	**30**	**35**
Conservative	$19.16	$23.83	$28.47	$33.05
Moderate	15.71	18.65	21.27	23.62
Aggressive	14.21	16.50	18.43	20.07

To use this table, Arnold must first determine how long he expects to live—and we already know he has selected age ninety. Because ninety is twenty-five years away from his current age of sixty-five, he would choose the 3.5 percent table and move to the vertical column labeled "twenty-five years."

Next, Arnold will have to select the investment strategy he plans to use. Because he is relatively inexperienced as an investor—but because he wants as large a return as he can get—he will choose the "moderate" line. The number he'll come up with is 16.04.

The rest is simple. Arnold should multiply the $13,200 income he wants by 16.04. The product is $211,728, or the amount he will need in principal to generate the $13,200 in inflation-adjusted annual income over a twenty-five-year period assuming a 3.5 percent rate of inflation. If you happen to be sixty-five or close to it right now, you can go through the same procedure to determine what you need.

The principal amount that Arnold requires may seem like a lot of money—but actually, he needs even more. I always recommend that my clients first figure out what they need in terms of income to live on, as Arnold has done. But then, they should plug in an *emergency fund* to protect themselves against certain crises or unexpected contingencies, such as increased medical care during the later years of life.

DO YOU REALLY NEED AN EMERGENCY FUND?

The advice I'm giving is based on the assumption that you will use up all your principal by the time you reach the age you have targeted as the end of your retirement. But what happens if you live a little longer than you planned? Or suppose you have unexpected medical expenses that aren't covered by Medicare or any insurance you may be carrying? Are nursing home expenses included in your insurance coverage—and if not, how are you going to pay them if you need ongoing care? How about your funeral expenses? Finally, do you want to leave any money to your heirs?

Any of these issues can make an emergency fund of some sort

appropriate—but how can you figure out how much you need and how you might save it up?

I usually suggest that the average person could provide some protection for himself with an emergency fund worth $50,000 *today*. That amount of money would go a long way toward defraying most serious medical expenses, or could keep you going for a few more years if you live longer than you expect.

The following chart shows how much Arnold—or you—would need to set aside in order to have the buying power of $50,000 in today's dollars twenty-five years from now.[5]

Table 3-7
$50,000 EMERGENCY NEST EGG GROWN OVER TWENTY-FIVE YEARS

Number of Years	$50,000* "Real" Nest Egg	Amount Needed		
		Investment Strategy		
		Conservative	Moderate	Aggressive
Initial Sum◊	50,000	**33,272**	**19,832**	**15,022**
1	51,750	35,002	21,300	16,314
2	53,561	36,822	22,876	17,717
3	55,436	38,737	24,569	19,241
4	57,376	40,751	26,387	20,895
5	59,384	42,870	28,340	22,692
6	61,462	45,099	30,437	24,644
7	63,613	47,445	32,689	26,763
8	65,839	49,912	35,108	29,065
9	68,143	52,507	37,706	31,564
10	70,528	55,238	40,496	34,279
11	72,996	58,110	43,493	37,227
12	75,551	61,132	46,711	40,428
13	78,195	64,310	50,168	43,905
14	80,932	67,655	53,880	47,681
15	83,765	71,173	57,868	51,781
16	86,697	74,874	62,150	56,235
17	89,731	78,767	66,749	61,071
18	92,872	82,863	71,688	66,323
19	96,123	87,172	76,993	72,027
20	99,487	91,705	82,691	78,221
21	102,969	96,473	88,810	84,948
22	106,573	101,490	95,382	92,253
23	110,303	106,767	102,440	100,187
24	114,164	112,319	110,020	108,803
25	118,160	118,160	118,162	118,160

Adjusted for inflation at 3.5% rate.

If Arnold prefers a conservative investment strategy, he would have to start out with $33,272 tomorrow to achieve his goal in twenty-five years. On the other hand, if he chooses an aggressive strategy, he would need only $15,022 tomorrow to achieve the same result. Using a moderate strategy, he would have to plan on starting out with $19,832 to reach his objective.

To sum up, then, in round numbers Arnold needs $211,000 to produce his $13,200 in inflation adjusted income, and about $20,000 to begin building his emergency fund—or a total of $231,000. And he needs the money *right now*. But how is he going to get it?

WHERE WILL ARNOLD GET THE EXTRA PRINCIPAL HE NEEDS?

Like many retirees, Arnold seems to have painted himself into a corner. He has waited until the last minute to plan for his retirement, and that has left him no leeway to build up his assets.

But fortunately for Arnold, there is a way out of this tight spot. First of all, he has reviewed his assets and discovered that he has a bit more than he remembered in his various savings accounts, including a small IRA fund that he has contributed to sporadically over the years. Second, he has built up a considerable amount of cash value in a whole life insurance policy he's been carrying for more than twenty years. And third, he owns his home—and the value has gone up considerably since he purchased it in the early 1970s.

Arnold wisely decides to leave his money in his IRA until the maximum age of seventy and a half, where it can continue to accumulate value in a tax-deferred status. He also decides to keep the cash value in his insurance policy for the time being because long-term interest rates are still relatively high—or at least are at a competitive level with many other fixed income investments he has been considering. He knows that he can still arrange his retirement finances so that he can draw income gradually from these investments as he needs it.

But Arnold still has a problem. Although the combined total from these two investments, the IRA and the insurance, comes to just over

$60,000, he is still short of the principal he needs by $171,000.

Again, there is an answer: Arnold can turn to his home equity. He has misgivings about selling his place because he's been there for so long, but maintenance costs have risen, and taxes are considerably higher than when he bought the property. The area where he lives happens to be in high demand by younger professionals and families with children who want to take advantage of the good schools in the vicinity. In other words, it's a seller's market. That means Arnold can get around $200,000 for his home, or more than he needs to make up the lump sum he's shooting for.

Finally, Arnold decides to sell his home, moves out of the popular suburban area where he has lived for so long, and takes an apartment about forty miles away in a nice complex with a swimming pool and other facilities.

Did Arnold make the right decision about selling his home and moving? Before we answer this question, let's personalize the issue by considering some of the factors that *you* should take into account before you make such a big decision.

What Should You Do with Your Home When You Retire?

Generally speaking, we view our homes as an investment. Whenever we complete a personal financial statement, we include the market value of our home as an asset and list the mortgage balance as a liability.

Of course, most of us buy a home for many reasons that have nothing to do with the property's investment potential. But even though there are many wonderful benefits and great feelings that go along with owning your own home, effective retirement planning requires that you control the emotional factors. Look more closely at your property as an asset that can be *used* to achieve a comfortable income after you quit work.

Assume that you are about to retire and you have paid off the mortgage on your $175,000 home. Assume further that your real estate taxes are $2,500 and your routine maintenance costs average $2,000 annually. This means that you have an asset that is worth $175,000, but will consume $4,500 per year of your retirement income. And that doesn't take into account major repairs, such as a new roof.

Another possibility is to sell your home—as Arnold decided to do—and either buy a much cheaper place or invest all your proceeds and rent. In most parts of the country, if you stay in the same area where your home is located, you can rent a nice apartment at a reasonable rate—perhaps $800 in a neighborhood with $175,000 homes. In this situation, your rent of $9,600 per year, less the $4,500 in housing expenses you would be saving, will leave you with an annual housing cost of $4,100. Most important, you will now have the net proceeds from the sale of your house to invest.

Assume that you net $150,000 after sales expenses, moving costs, and taxes. (Assume also that you take advantage of the one-time federal tax exemption for housing of $125,000—which would greatly lower any capital gains tax you may owe.) You could then invest the $150,000 in a diversified portfolio of mutual funds, with a relatively moderate 7 to 8 percent long-term annual investment objective. If your mutual funds produce an average 8 percent return, you could find yourself in great financial shape.

Let's suppose you withdraw 2.7 percent of the 8 percent return each year from these funds to cover the $4,100 you need to pay your rent. Also, you leave 2 percent worth of the return in the fund to enable the fund principal to keep growing. This would leave you with the remaining 3.3 percent of the investment return as extra retirement income, or $5,000 a year!

The economics of home ownership is clear. If your retirement nest egg is inadequate or marginal, you should seriously consider turning your home equity into an income-producing asset. Most people make the mistake of thinking it is less expensive to continue living in a home they have paid off because they don't have to pay rent every month. But it's easy to underestimate the cost of home ownership.

So go through your records for the past two or three years, and determine how much money you have pumped into your home. Include everything: insurance, taxes, lawn care, routine maintenance, etc. You may be surprised at the total. Then, factor in what you can earn on your reinvested home equity. You may find there is no comparison between renting and owning a home. Renting often wins hands down.

Now let's return to Arnold's final retirement plans. There is still one issue he needs to take into account as he figures out how much principal will produce adequate income in the future—and that issue is taxes.

TAXES ON RETIREMENT INCOME

Unfortunately, taxes do not go away when you retire. If your retirement nest egg is sitting in a tax-sheltered account such as an IRA, you will have to pay federal income taxes—and state and city taxes when applicable—on the full amount you withdraw each year. The investment income you earn on the assets that remain *inside* your IRA, however, will continue to be tax-sheltered.

If you have been accumulating your nest egg outside of a tax-sheltered arrangement, such as in a regular brokerage account or bank, you will have to pay tax on the investment income you realize, plus any capital gains you earn.

Also, you will have to pay taxes on your Social Security benefits if your "adjusted income" exceeds certain threshold amounts. "Adjusted income" refers to your adjusted gross income as determined for federal income taxes, tax-free interest, one-half of Social Security benefits, and designated income from foreign sources.

According to current federal rules, if you are single and your "adjusted income" exceeds $25,000 a year (but is less than $34,000), you have to pay taxes on one-half of your Social Security benefits. In Arnold's case, the Social Security component of his annual retirement income of $30,000 would just miss being taxed because his "adjusted income" would be less than $25,000.

If you are single with an adjusted income above $34,000, you would be hit with an even higher levy by being taxed on 85 percent of your Social Security income. Married taxpayers must pay taxes on 50 percent of their Social Security benefits when their combined adjusted income exceeds $32,000, and on 85 percent when they pass an adjusted income level of $44,000.

Finally, you may have to pay capital gains taxes on the sale of your primary residence if:

- you are younger than fifty-five,
- you are over fifty-five but have already used up your $125,000 housing exemption, or
- you are over fifty-five and have not used up your $125,000 exemption, but you realize a profit of more than $125,000, over and above the cost basis of your house.

You will note that I have not commented on the taxes Arnold will have to pay on his retirement income. Arnold will need a retirement income that is equal to 70 to 80 percent of his gross income when he retires, rather than 70 to 80 percent of his after-tax income. I have assumed that Arnold's entire retirement income will be taxable when he retires.

Most of your retirement income is likely to come from sources that will be taxable. These include an employer provided pension, 401(k), 403(b), 457, and IRA benefits. I also recommend expecting 100 percent of any Social Security benefits you receive to be taxable. If you sell your home and reinvest the amount you receive, you will be required to pay tax on interest, dividends, and realized capital gains. The bottom line is not to expect a tax break after you retire.

WHAT LESSONS CAN YOU LEARN
FROM ARNOLD'S RETIREMENT EXPERIENCE?

Regardless of how old you are right now, there are several lessons to be learned from Arnold's encounter with retirement planning.

Lesson one: Expect to live at least to age ninety. If you limit your planning to your statistical life expectancy, you may miss the mark and set yourself up for trouble.

Lesson two: Identify all your potential sources of retirement income—and use them shrewdly. Arnold drew income from a wide variety of sources common to many of us: Social Security, a defined benefit pension plan, IRA savings fund, non-tax-sheltered personal savings, insurance cash values, and home equity.

Lesson three: Always plug in a cost-of-living increase when you are projecting the income you will need many years into the future. Arnold figured in a 3.5 percent annual inflation rate, a reasonable assumption for most people.

Lesson four: Always anticipate the taxes you think you may have to pay when you are trying to determine the income you think you'll need for a comfortable retirement. Be sure that you think in terms of your *net*, after-tax income before you finalize your goal amount.

Lesson five: Employ at least a moderate investment strategy for your retirement investments. If you try to rely on a strategy that is too conservative, you will either run out of money too early, or you will have to start off with a considerably larger sum to meet your retirement income needs.

Obviously, there are many advantages to the moderate or aggressive strategies. So if, like Arnold, you find yourself strapped for cash—and retirement has crept up on you before you have taken time to do much planning—you should definitely steer clear of the conservative approach.

Lesson six: Don't wait until you are sixty-five to begin your retirement planning! Of course, Arnold didn't have a choice because he was already sixty-five and if you are in that situation, you can learn a great deal about a last-minute marshaling of your assets from the approach he took. But it's obviously better to begin to lay the groundwork for your retirement when you are much younger. That's what the individuals described in the following pages did—and as a result, they should be much better prepared than Arnold was when the time arrives for them to quit work for good.

NOTES

1. See the table entitled "What You Can Expect Today in Social Security Benefits" on page 197 of the appendix, which gives you an idea of the Social Security payments that single and married people at different ages and income levels can expect to receive if they retire today.

2. For the sake of simplicity, I have omitted a discussion of whether or not a cost-of-living increase would be included in Arnold's pension income. Here, I am assuming that such an

annual increase *would* be part of Arnold's pension payment—though many times these increases are not part of a defined benefit pension package. As far as Social Security payments are concerned, cost-of-living increases are currently included—though with the recent movement to cut government costs, these increases may be reduced or phased out in the future.

For example, Federal Reserve Chairman Alan Greenspan has testified that the Social Security cost-of-living adjustments substantially exceed the actual cost-of-living increases. That is good ammunition to argue for reducing the current cost-of-living adjustments that are made in Social Security payments.

3. The rates of return I have selected for the conservative, moderate, and aggressive strategies I've described are based on average annual returns from 1926 through 1993.
4. To see how you would manage your nest egg over periods of twenty years and thirty years at the three levels of return, see the additional charts in the appendix.
5. To see how much it would take to put together a $50,000 emergency nest egg over a period of twenty years and thirty years, see the additional charts in the appendix.

CHAPTER FOUR

THE FOUR BASIC RETIREMENT SCENARIOS

NUTS AND BOLTS PLANNING
FOR A SECURE FUTURE

n my research on retirement, I have identified four basic "retirement scenarios" which have served as models of effective investment planning.

Scenario 1: The person who plans to retire immediately.
Scenario 2: The thirty-five-year-old who plans to retire at sixty-five.
Scenario 3: The forty-five-year-old who plans to retire at sixty-five.
Scenario 4: The fifty-five-year-old who plans to retire at sixty-five.

If you don't fit exactly into one of the above age categories (e.g., you're forty-two or fifty-three), that won't matter because you will be taught how to calculate your retirement needs no matter how old you are right now. The key to these calculations involves learning how to use four basic tables.

HOW TO USE THE FOUR KEY TABLES IN EACH PERSONAL
RETIREMENT SCENARIO

The four basic retirement scenarios revolve around four key tables, two of which were introduced in chapter 3. If you understand how to use these tables, your own planning will become a snap. Here is an explanation of what the tables contain and how they work.

Table 4-1: The Amount Needed to Provide One Dollar of Inflation-Adjusted Income After Retirement

Remember, throughout this book, the first assumption you will make is that you will retire *tomorrow*. So you will need to know (1) how much retirement income you would need beginning tomorrow, and also (2) how large a nest egg you would need to provide that income in *today's dollars* until the moment you die.

Table 4-1 (shown on page 80) provides you with factors that enable you to find what it will take to generate $1.00 of inflation-adjusted income over different retirement periods, at different inflation rates, and with different investment strategies. As mentioned in the previous chapter, I'll assume that *after* retirement, a "conservative" strategy will produce a 5.2 percent average annual rate of return; a "moderate" strategy will mean a 7.4 percent rate; and an "aggressive" strategy will involve an 8.6 percent rate.

Table 4-2: The Inflation Adjustment Table

You will use this table (shown on page 81) to adjust your retirement nest egg for the rise in cost of living that will occur between now and the time you actually retire. So suppose that you plan to retire thirty years from now, and you assume there will be a 3.5 percent inflation rate. This table gives you the factors to multiply your nest egg by in order to get the actual inflation-adjusted principal you will need at retirement.

Table 4-3: Table for Projecting Current Savings Before Retirement

You will use this chart (shown on page 82) to determine how much your current savings will be worth at retirement after a given number of years, using one of the three main investment strategies. All you have to do is take the total amount you have saved so far and multiply that by the appropriate factor in the table. In this table it's assumed that other than the return on investment, no money is added to or sub-tracted from this savings amount.

Table 4-4: Table for Projecting Accumulation of Future Savings Before Retirement

This table (shown on page 83) will enable you to figure out how much money you will have to save each year to end up with the nest egg you need. You'll just divide an appropriate factor taken from this chart into the amount you will need to accumulate by retirement age.

Table 4-1

AMOUNT NEEDED TO PROVIDE ONE DOLLAR
OF INFLATION-ADJUSTED INCOME AFTER RETIREMENT

Inflation Rate—3.0%			
Investment Strategy	**Number of Years Income Will Be Needed**		
	20	**25**	**30**	**35**
Conservative	$16.08	$19.14	$21.90	$24.38
Moderate	13.36	15.29	16.85	18.12
Aggressive	12.16	13.67	14.82	15.71

Inflation Rate—3.5%			
Investment Strategy	**Number of Years Income Will Be Needed**		
	20	**25**	**30**	**35**
Conservative	$16.78	$20.19	$23.33	$26.23
Moderate	13.91	16.04	17.82	19.30
Aggressive	12.64	14.31	15.62	16.65

Inflation Rate—4.0%			
Investment Strategy	**Number of Years Income Will Be Needed**		
	20	**25**	**30**	**35**
Conservative	$17.53	$21.32	$24.90	$28.25
Moderate	14.47	16.85	18.88	20.61
Aggressive	13.13	14.99	16.48	17.69

Inflation Rate—4.5%			
Investment Strategy	**Number of Years Income Will Be Needed**		
	20	**25**	**30**	**35**
Conservative	$18.32	$22.53	$26.60	$30.54
Moderate	15.08	17.72	20.03	22.04
Aggressive	13.66	15.72	17.42	18.82

Inflation Rate—5.0%			
Investment Strategy	**Number of Years Income Will Be Needed**		
	20	**25**	**30**	**35**
Conservative	$19.16	$23.83	$28.47	$33.05
Moderate	15.71	18.65	21.27	23.62
Aggressive	14.21	16.50	18.43	20.07

Table 4-2
INFLATION ADJUSTMENT TABLE

Number of Years	Assumed Annual Rate of Change				
	3%	*3.5%*	*4%*	*4.5%*	*5%*
1	1.03	1.035	1.04	1.045	1.05
2	1.06	1.07	1.08	1.09	1.10
3	1.09	1.11	1.12	1.14	1.16
4	1.13	1.15	1.17	1.19	1.22
5	1.16	1.19	1.22	1.25	1.28
6	1.19	1.23	1.27	1.30	1.34
7	1.23	1.27	1.32	1.36	1.41
8	1.27	1.32	1.37	1.42	1.48
9	1.30	1.36	1.42	1.49	1.55
10	1.34	1.41	1.48	1.55	1.63
11	1.38	1.46	1.54	1.62	1.71
12	1.43	1.51	1.60	1.70	1.80
13	1.47	1.56	1.67	1.77	1.89
14	1.51	1.62	1.73	1.85	1.98
15	1.56	1.68	1.80	1.94	2.08
16	1.60	1.73	1.87	2.02	2.18
17	1.65	1.79	1.95	2.11	2.29
18	1.70	1.86	2.03	2.21	2.41
19	1.75	1.92	2.11	2.31	2.53
20	1.81	1.99	2.19	2.41	2.65
21	1.86	2.06	2.28	2.52	2.79
22	1.92	2.13	2.37	2.63	2.93
23	1.97	2.21	2.46	2.75	3.07
24	2.03	2.28	2.56	2.88	3.23
25	2.09	2.36	2.67	3.01	3.39
26	2.16	2.45	2.77	3.14	3.56
27	2.22	2.53	2.88	3.28	3.73
28	2.29	2.62	3.00	3.43	3.92
29	2.36	2.71	3.12	3.58	4.12
30	2.43	2.81	3.24	3.75	4.32

Table 4-3
TABLE FOR PROJECTING CURRENT SAVINGS BEFORE RETIREMENT

Years	Investment Strategy		
	Conservative	*Moderate*	*Aggressive*
1	1.062	1.086	1.103
2	1.128	1.179	1.217
3	1.198	1.281	1.342
4	1.272	1.391	1.480
5	1.351	1.511	1.633
6	1.435	1.641	1.801
7	1.524	1.782	1.986
8	1.618	1.935	2.191
9	1.718	2.101	2.416
10	1.825	2.282	2.665
11	1.938	2.478	2.939
12	2.058	2.691	3.242
13	2.186	2.923	3.576
14	2.321	3.174	3.944
15	2.465	3.447	4.351
16	2.618	3.743	4.799
17	2.780	4.065	5.293
18	2.953	4.415	5.839
19	3.136	4.795	6.440
20	3.330	5.207	7.103
21	3.537	5.655	7.835
22	3.756	6.141	8.642
23	3.989	6.669	9.532
24	4.236	7.243	10.514
25	4.499	7.866	11.597
26	4.778	8.542	12.791
27	5.074	9.277	14.109
28	5.389	10.075	15.562
29	5.723	10.941	17.165
30	6.078	11.882	18.933

Table 4-4
TABLE FOR PROJECTING ACCUMULATION OF FUTURE RETIREMENT SAVINGS BEFORE RETIREMENT

	Investment Strategy		
Years	*Conservative*	*Moderate*	*Aggressive*
1	1.000	1.000	1.000
2	2.062	2.086	2.103
3	3.190	3.265	3.320
4	4.388	4.546	4.662
5	5.660	5.937	6.142
6	7.011	7.448	7.774
7	8.445	9.088	9.575
8	9.969	10.870	11.561
9	11.587	12.805	13.752
10	13.305	14.906	16.168
11	15.130	17.188	18.834
12	17.068	19.666	21.774
13	19.126	22.357	25.016
14	21.312	25.280	28.593
15	23.634	28.454	32.538
16	26.099	31.901	36.890
17	28.717	35.645	41.689
18	31.498	39.710	46.983
19	34.450	44.125	52.823
20	37.586	48.920	59.263
21	40.917	54.127	66.367
22	44.454	59.782	74.203
23	48.210	65.923	82.846
24	52.199	72.592	92.379
25	56.435	79.835	102.894
26	60.934	87.701	114.493
27	65.712	96.244	127.285
28	70.786	105.521	141.396
29	76.175	115.595	156.959
30	81.898	126.536	174.126

The above factors are how much $1.00 invested each year will grow to over the applicable number of future years assuming the investment performance for each investment strategy equals historical returns achieved during the period from 1926 through 1993. It has been assumed that the amount you save does not earn any investment income during the year it is invested. This will understate your actual results if you invest the entire amount at the beginning of the year or periodically during the year.

Now, let's move directly to the practical application of these tables in each of the basic retirement scenarios. Regardless of how old you are now, I would suggest that you look at *all* the scenarios in this chapter. The more experience you have in handling the tables and the planning procedures in real-life situations, the more adept you will become in designing your own personal retirement program.

SCENARIO ONE:
THE PERSON WHO PLANS TO RETIRE IMMEDIATELY

We've already discussed the first individual—sixty-five-year-old Arnold who planned to retire "tomorrow." I'll be referring to him and his concerns periodically throughout the book because, as I've said, the "retire-tomorrow" assumption should be the starting point in planning for *anyone*, regardless of age or family situation. But we won't retread Arnold all over again in this chapter. Just remember that he was our first scenario—and use his approach if you happen to be in his situation.

Now, let's turn to the second scenario: the thirty-five-year-old who plans to retire at age sixty-five. For the sake of simplicity, I'll assume throughout the scenarios in this chapter—as I have in earlier illustrations in this book—that you have a working income of about $40,000, and a retirement income of $30,000. Later, in chapter 7, I will be assuming for comparison's sake considerably higher working incomes of $60,000 and $100,000. But don't fixate too much on the dollar figures we're dealing with here. Regardless of what your income may actually be, the basic principles and procedures for achieving retirement objectives still apply.

SCENARIO TWO:
RETIREMENT PLANNING FOR THE THIRTY-FIVE-YEAR-OLD

If you are now thirty-five years old, and you earn $40,000, what will it take for you to be able to retire thirty years from now, at sixty-five? If you start by assuming you are going to retire tomorrow, and you think you'll need 75 percent of your $40,000 salary, you need to plan to achieve an annual $30,000 income.

Assume further that you do not expect to receive a traditional monthly pension from an employer. You either currently work for a company that doesn't offer a defined benefit pension plan, or you don't expect to work in the future for such an employer.

How about Social Security? Most thirty-five-year-olds I know don't count on receiving any Social Security benefits—and most surveys of people in this age group confirm my observations about these attitudes. So for the time being, let's assume that you won't get any Social Security.

In this illustration and those that follow in this chapter, I won't factor in the $50,000 emergency fund we discussed in chapter 3. But I do recommend that everyone have such a fund, and I would suggest that you include it in your retirement planning.

So you are left in this position: You have to accumulate a nest egg to provide the *entire* $30,000 retirement income you would need if you were retiring tomorrow. That's quite a large order—and a powerful, systematic program is required to fulfill it. The following step-by-step procedure should give you all the tools you need to plan toward your ultimate objective of retiring comfortably thirty years from now.

Step one: Determine how large a nest egg you would need to generate the income required for you to retire tomorrow.

To take this step, you need to answer the following questions:

■ How long do I expect to live after I retire?
  Answer: Twenty-five years, to age ninety.

■ What is the annual inflation rate likely to be after I retire?
  Answer: An average of 3.5 percent per year.

■ What kind of investment strategy will I use with my nest egg during my retirement years?
  Answer: You will use a moderate investment strategy *after* retirement—though you may choose another approach before you reach retirement age. Also, you will plan on using up all your principal so that you have nothing left at age ninety.

Now refer to table 4-1 on page 80. You will choose the factor 16.04 from the 3.5 percent chart and multiply that by the retirement income you need, $30,000. The result is a nest egg of $481,200—the amount of principal you would need if you were going to retire tomorrow.

But in reality, you are not going to retire tomorrow. You won't say goodbye to the working world until thirty years from now. If the cost of living between now and then increases at an average annual rate of 3.5 percent, you'll actually need a great deal larger principal to generate the equivalent of $30,000 today.

To find out how large, look at table 4-2 on page 81. Multiply the $481,200, which you know you would need to generate $30,000 of income today, by 2.81, which is the thirty-year factor for a 3.5 percent increase. The product, $1,352,172, is the amount of principal you would need to generate $30,000 of *inflation-adjusted* annual income, which would begin thirty years from now, and would continue for another twenty-five years, until age ninety.

Step two: Establish and follow a strategy to accumulate the retirement nest egg you will need. There are only two ways to "grow" the money you will need: (1) increase the size of contributions you and your employers make to retirement funds, and (2) increase the rate of return on your investments. You must strike the right balance between these two factors to achieve your ultimate objectives.

Remember that when you are planning your investment strategy *before* retirement, you have to think in terms of higher returns—both because you can afford to take more risk, and you need to accumulate as much as possible by the time you quit work. So in this working stage of your life, "conservative" means a 6.2 percent annual return; "moderate" refers to an 8.6 percent return; and "aggressive" involves a 10.3 percent average annual return.

Let's assume that at age thirty-five you have already saved something toward retirement—say, $15,000. The first thing you should do in trying to settle on your personal long-term investment approach is to determine how much that sum will be worth at the time of your retirement. And that value will depend on which of the three possible investment strategies you use. Refer to table 4-3 on page 82 throughout the following discussion.

The Conservative Strategy

If you decide to shoot for only a 6.2 percent return per year between now and your retirement age of sixty-five, choose the thirty-year factor from the conservative column on the chart—or 6.078. Now, multiply this factor by your current investment balance of $15,000. This would give you $91,170 at age sixty-five.

If you subtract this amount from $1,352,172, which is the total principal you know you need to generate to get your $30,000 of annual inflation-adjusted income, you'll end up with $1,261,002. This is the amount you'll have to accumulate by age sixty-five.

The best way to do so is to invest a certain amount of money at a certain rate every year—either on your own or through an employer contributory plan like the 401(k). How much money are we talking about?

If you expect to pursue a conservative investment strategy, you'll need to put in $15,397 each year. You come up with this amount by taking the total amount you need to accumulate—$1,261,002—and dividing it by the factor 81.898, which is the factor on the thirty-year line at the bottom of the "conservative" strategy column on table 4-4 (page 83). This will give you the $15,397 that you must put in every year—which amounts to a huge 38 percent of your $40,000 salary.

It's not likely that on a $40,000 a year income, you would be able to set aside this much money, especially not if you have family obligations, such as paying for your child's college tuition. So what are your other options? The first thing I would suggest is to adjust your investment strategy to enable you to get a higher return on your principal every year.

The Moderate Strategy

A worker in his thirties, who has no other source of retirement income, should not be using a conservative investment strategy. You may sleep well now because you are a "safe" investor who experiences little up or down movement from month to month or year to year in the value of your assets. But you are taking a big risk that you will lie awake years from now because you have not accumulated enough money to retire.

Let's see what happens if you decide to take a few more risks by following the moderate strategy. First, find the thirty-year factor for a moderate strategy on table 4-3. That factor is 11.882, which you would then multiply by the $15,000 we are assuming you have already saved. That would give you an expected accumulation on those savings of $178,230 by age sixty-five. Next, you must find the *additional* amount you will need to accumulate over the next thirty years. So you subtract the $178,230 from the total of $1,352,172 that you know you must have in order to generate $30,000 worth of annual inflation-adjusted income by age sixty-five. The result is $1,173,942.

To accumulate this amount within thirty years by using a moderate investment strategy, you would have to save $9,278 each year. Again, you arrive at this figure by referring to table 4-4 and finding the factor for thirty years in the "moderate" investment strategy column. Then you divide that factor, 126.536, into the $1,173,942 total you must accumulate to give you the $9,278 that you have to save each year.

This savings figure, which represents 23 percent of your current $40,000 annual salary, is considerably better than the 38 percent you would have to set aside with the conservative strategy. But you're still looking at a lot of money here—probably considerably more than you feel you can manage. So let's try the third investment option—the aggressive approach.

The Aggressive Strategy

Using an aggressive investment strategy before retirement, you would expect to generate an average annual return of 10.3 percent—a hefty amount that could probably be achieved only by a portfolio that is 100 percent in stocks. At some points in different economic and investing cycles, "junk" bonds, which have a relatively low rating but a high yield, may be an alternative for the aggressive portfolio. But historically, over a period of several decades, investing in common stocks has proven to be the only way to achieve average annual gains in excess of 10 percent.

With this aggressive approach, you would first multiply your $15,000 savings by the factor 18.933 on the thirty-year line of the "aggressive" column in table 4-3. That would give you $283,955 by the time you are sixty-five. Then, you would subtract that amount from the total $1,352,172 you need. The result, $1,068,217, is the principal you need to accumulate over the next thirty years. To determine the annual amount you would have to invest to accumulate that much money, you would turn once more to table 4-4. On the thirty-year line under the "aggressive" column is the factor 174.126. Divide that into the $1,068,217 to get $6,135—which is what your annual contribution would have to be.

At 15 percent of your annual income, this is still a large sum to save every year, but it can be done. Some people, who have to save all the money themselves, succeed by cutting back on their expenses. A less painful approach is possible for those who have a 401(k) retirement savings plan or a similar program, where the employer matches employee contributions. For example, if your employer has agreed to match your contributions dollar for dollar, you would need to put in only *half* of the annual amount you need, or a little over $3,000 per year. That would represent only about 7.5 percent of your salary—still a substantial amount, but quite possible for most people.

If you feel that hiking your savings to this extent is simply too burdensome, there are some other options you might try—as indicated in step 3.

Step three: Identify some secondary strategies—if investment returns alone won't produce the desired income. Remember that we started this example for a thirty-five-year-old by assuming that there would be no future Social Security or traditional pension benefits. But the odds are that there will be *some* income from one or both of these sources, even if the amount isn't as much as you might like.

Assume that if you retired today, you would qualify for an annual Social Security payment of $14,000.[1] But because Social Security benefits are likely to be reduced in the future, I would advise you to count on benefits of no more than 50 percent of the current payments, or $7,000 in today's dollars. Still, even this greatly reduced amount would be a welcome addition to your retirement income.

Now, assume that you also qualify for traditional defined benefit pensions that will pay you another $3,000 a year in today's dollars when you retire. This amount, plus the Social Security, would give you $10,000 a year, or 33 percent of the $30,000 retirement income you will need.

In other words, the total principal you would now have to pull together over the next thirty years has been reduced by 33 percent from $1,352,172 to $901,453.

Using the various tables and procedures we have employed earlier in this chapter, you would find that with a moderate investment strategy, you would now have to accumulate only $723,223 in future savings ($901,453 minus $178,230) by age sixty-five. You could do this by saving only $5,716 each year—or 14 percent of your annual salary. And if you are in a matching 401(k) program with your employer, the amount and percentage you would have to contribute would be much less.

Another strategy you could use to improve your retirement picture is to plan to work beyond age sixty-five. If you put in another five years—or even two or three—you will increase the amount of income you make and the contributions you can put into your retirement fund. Also, you will postpone the time at which you begin to withdraw money from your retirement account.

An additional consideration is that since you are only thirty-five years old, your income will most likely go up in the future at a rate faster than the cost of living. I've been assuming a 3.5 percent increase in the cost of living *and* your income, but your income may actually increase at a 4 percent rate, or even more. If this happens, you should increase the percentage of your income that is saved for retirement.

The thirty-five-year-old who follows the general outlines of the three-part strategy I've presented in this chapter should be in good shape by the time he or she reaches sixty-five. If you are married and have a working spouse, your chances are even better for reaching your retirement goals because you'll have more income (more on this later in this chapter). Whatever your family circumstances, however, you must guard against becoming complacent. As you plan for the future, always remember:

- It's essential to start saving for retirement now. Don't wait!
- Get your savings rate up to 10 percent or more of your before-tax salary.
- After you identify the annual amount you must save to reach your goals, put in that amount *every year*, without fail. Consistency and discipline are the keys to successful retirement planning.
- When you switch jobs, always take retirement and other benefits into consideration. Can you qualify for extra benefits by staying on at one company a little longer—without jeopardizing your opportunities to move into a new position? Can you negotiate a little harder to improve your retirement benefits at your new company?
- Resist being a conservative investor. Always use at least a moderate investment strategy. This point becomes even more important if you don't expect to receive a substantial portion of your retirement benefits from an employer-provided pension.

At age thirty-five, you still have plenty of time to prepare effectively for retirement. And as we'll see in chapter 7, by working hard at your personal investing you may even be able to retire earlier than age sixty-five. But the longer you wait, the fewer your options. You'll begin to see how the options shrink as we explore our next scenario—the retirement strategy for the person who begins planning at age forty-five.

SCENARIO THREE:
RETIREMENT PLANNING FOR THE FORTY-FIVE-YEAR-OLD

If you are now forty-five years old, the retirement challenges you face—and the procedures to deal with those challenges—are essentially the same as for the thirty-five-year-old, except for the obvious: You have ten fewer years to accumulate what you need.

Let's assume once again that you are now earning $40,000 annually and that your targeted retirement age is sixty-five. If you were to retire immediately, you would need at least 75 percent of your current salary, or $30,000. Also, you expect to live for twenty-five years after retirement, or until you are ninety years old.

But unlike the previous scenario, this time you do expect to receive a traditional pension from one or more of your employers. Specifically, you anticipate receiving pension payments equal to 12.5 percent of your final salary—or $5,000 per year in today's dollars.

Also, because of the likelihood of reduced Social Security benefits in the future, you expect to receive Social Security payments equal to 50 percent of what is currently projected as your Social Security benefit. According to present rules, if you retired right now, you would get Social Security benefits of about $14,000 a year.[2] So, according to our assumptions, you would get half of that at sixty-five, or $7,000 a year.

The annual amount you would get from your pension, plus your Social Security payments, would add up to $12,000. That leaves you with an additional $18,000 in inflation-adjusted income you have to generate each year. How do you achieve this objective?

First of all, you should determine the size of the nest egg you would need to generate $18,000 a year if you retired tomorrow. To do this, you multiply your desired extra income of $18,000 by the factor 16.04, which you can find on table 4-1. (Look under the "25-year" column, on the "moderate" investment strategy line.) This product is $288,720— or the amount of principal you would need to generate your inflation-adjusted $18,000 annual income.

Again, I'm assuming a 3.5 percent inflation rate during the twenty-five years you plan to spend in retirement, and I'm assuming that you'll employ a moderate investment strategy during your retirement years. If you want to make different assumptions, you can do so by choosing another factor from table 4-1.

You know from this initial calculation that you need $288,720 to produce $18,000 income at the present time. But you still have twenty years to go until you reach age sixty-five—and you can expect inflation to continue during that period. So let's assume that an annual 3.5 percent increase in your retirement income of $18,000 would be necessary during this twenty-year period.

To achieve this goal, find the factor 1.99 in the 3.5 percent column on the twenty-year line in table 4-2. Multiply this factor by the $288,720 nest egg you need today. The product is $574,553, the amount of principal you would need to accumulate by age sixty-five.

Another assumption we'll make here is that at age forty-five, you have been saving for retirement long enough to have accumulated $50,000. If you can get a decent investment return on this sum during the next twenty years, you will go a long way toward covering the total principal you'll need when you retire. Here are some of the possible strategies for growing your $50,000 nest egg between now and the time you retire, using the conservative, moderate, and aggressive portfolio strategies.

The Conservative Strategy

Find the 3.33 factor on the twenty-year line in table 4-3 and multiply your $50,000 savings by that to get $166,500—the amount your current savings would be worth at the time you retire.

Next, subtract this amount from the total principal you will need—$574,553—to get $408,053, which is the extra amount you still must accumulate. How much would you have to save each year to reach this goal? Again, look at table 4-4 and find the factor 37.586 under the "conservative" column on the twenty-year line. Divide that into the $408,053 you still need to accumulate, and you'll discover that you'll have to save $10,857 per year—a hefty 27 percent—out of your $40,000 salary.

The Moderate Strategy

To ease the financial pressure you would face with the conservative approach, try shooting for an average annual investment return of 8.6 percent instead. The procedure is exactly the same.

First, find the potential value of your $50,000 savings at age sixty-five by multiplying it by 5.207, the twenty-year factor in the moderate column on table 4-3. The product is $260,350. Next, subtract that amount from $574,553 to get the amount you will have left to accumulate—$314,203. Then, relying on table 4-4, divide that amount by 48.920, to get $6,423, which is the annual amount you must save each year to reach your objective. Certainly, this is a significant amount to have to put away—16 percent of your salary—but if you are in a program like a 401(k) where your employer is matching your contributions, you can probably manage it.

The Aggressive Strategy

If you achieve an average 10.3 annual return on your $50,000 investment, you could have $355,150 in twenty years. This figure is the product of multiplying the $50,000 by the factor 7.103 in the "aggressive" column on the twenty-year line in table 4-3. That would leave you with only $219,403 additional principal to accumulate between now and your retirement.

To find the annual amount you would have to save over the next twenty years, turn to table 4-4 on page 83. Divide the factor 59.263, which is in the "aggressive" column on the twenty-year line, into the extra $219,403 you will need at age sixty-five. The result, $3,702, is the amount you'll have to save each year to reach your goal. That represents only 9 percent of your $40,000 salary, and much less might come out of your pocket if your employer offers a matching-funds retirement savings arrangement.

So where do you stand? Clearly, if you are now forty-five years old, you are not likely to be able to retire comfortably at age sixty-five unless:

- You have already accumulated a substantial retirement savings fund.
- You will receive a significant pension or other form of retirement income from an employer.
- You are following a moderate or aggressive investment strategy.

- You will have other assets that can be used to provide retirement income—such as inheritance from parents, or equity in a home.

Let's suppose you own a home that will be paid off by the time you are sixty-five. As we saw in the story of Arnold in the previous chapter, you could sell your home and invest the proceeds to generate additional investment income.

For example, if you expect your home to be worth $200,000 when you sell it at age sixty-five, you could use the moderate investment model to reduce the nest egg you have to accumulate from $314,203 to $114,203. The annual amount you would have to save would then go down to $2,334, or 5.8 percent of your salary.

Whatever your current situation at age forty-five, you must act consistently, with discipline, in following your retirement plan. You have twenty years to go, but that time will quickly evaporate—as the person who is fifty-five years old already knows.

SCENARIO FOUR:
RETIREMENT PLANNING FOR THE FIFTY-FIVE-YEAR-OLD

At age fifty-five, if you want to retire in ten years, you should be well on the road to meeting your retirement objectives. In this scenario, we'll assume once more that you're single, your salary is $40,000, and you will need $30,000 of annual income in today's dollars when you retire.

Now, assume once again that you are going to retire tomorrow and that you'll receive a traditional pension equal to 15 percent of your final salary, or $6,000 per year. You also expect to receive Social Security benefits equal to 75 percent of what is currently projected as your Social Security benefit. This means you would get payments of $10,350 per year.[3]

The pension plus the Social Security would give you a total of $16,350, leaving you with the challenge of generating $13,650 in today's dollars to cover your annual retirement income of $30,000 ten years from now. To move through your planning sequence, remember first to assume that you are already sixty-five, and you are retiring immediately. How large of a nest egg would you need right now to generate an annual inflation-adjusted income of $13,650 for the next twenty-five years? (Again, assume an annual cost of living increase of 3.5 percent.)

To find this basic retirement nest egg amount, consult table 4-1 and choose the factor 16.04. Then multiply 16.04 by the income you need to achieve by retirement—$13,650—and that will give you your target nest egg of $218,946.

Next, come back to the present and your current age of fifty-five. Assume that your income will have to increase by an average of 3.5 percent a year over the next ten years in order to cover cost-of-living rises during that period. This means that you will have to take your $218,946 retirement nest egg and multiply it by the factor 1.41 on the ten-year line of table 4-2. The result is $308,714—which is the amount you will have to accumulate by age sixty-five.

The next step in your planning is to evaluate your current savings and assets. We will assume that you have a total savings of $80,000 so far. To see how much this will be worth in ten years according to the three different investment strategies, you will once more use table 4-3 and table 4-4.

The Conservative Strategy

Using the conservative investment approach before retirement (6.2 percent return), your $80,000 savings would increase to $146,000 in ten years (multiply the factor 1.825 from table 4-3 by $80,000). This would leave you with $162,714 left to accumulate (the total required nest egg of $308,714 minus the $146,000 you've already saved).

To determine the amount of money you would have to save each year for the next ten years, divide the factor 13.305 from table 4-4 into the $162,714 you need to accumulate. Your required annual savings is $12,230. That would represent a huge bite out of your annual income of $40,000 (31 percent), so let's try again.

The Moderate Strategy

The moderate investment strategy (8.6 percent) would bring your $80,000 savings up to $182,560 in ten years ($80,000 times the factor 2.282 from table 4-3). That would leave you with $126,154 to accumulate by age sixty-five. To achieve this goal, you would have to save $8,463 each year for the next ten years (divide $126,154 by 14.906 from table 4-4). That is 21 percent of your $40,000 salary—again, a very large proportion of your earnings.

The Aggressive Strategy

The aggressive strategy (10.3 percent return) would increase your $80,000 savings to $213,200 in ten years (multiply the factor 2.665 from table 4-3 by $80,000). When you subtract $213,200 from the $308,714 total nest egg you would need, you get $95,514—the amount you have to accumulate before age sixty-five. The amount you'll have to save each year is $5,908 (divide the factor 16.168 from table 4-4 into $95,514). That represents 15 percent of your salary—again, a large percentage of your total earnings.

Clearly, even with the higher nest egg that you have amassed *and* larger Social Security payments, it's much harder to accumulate the amount of money you need at age fifty-five than it was at the younger ages.

Even so, I would *not* recommend that you use the aggressive investment strategy when you are in your mid-fifties. The risk is too great that you may incur a heavy loss in your portfolio without having sufficient time to recover. The moderate investment strategy is preferable for you. But what if you just can't save 21 percent of your salary?

Other options would be to dip into your home equity or perhaps even the cash value of your insurance policies. But remember: Anything you take out of the savings portion of a whole life insurance policy will be deducted from the benefit paid to your beneficiaries. Also, you may find that your premiums go up because you will have lower insurance dividends being applied against them.

The main point to keep in mind is this: If you are in your fifties when you begin any serious retirement planning, you almost certainly will have to set aside a higher portion of your income to "catch up" in your capital accumulation than if you had started earlier. So bite the bullet and get started *immediately*!

SPECIAL CONSIDERATIONS FOR COUPLES

Whether you are single or married hasn't been a major consideration for most of what you have read so far, but there are some special issues related to marriage that you should keep in mind as you plan for retirement.

First of all, a couple can certainly save more money by living together than they could if they were two independent individuals living apart. The most obvious savings are in housing. Still, two *cannot* live as cheaply as one. Just having two mouths to feed or two people to go to the movies instead of one will automatically hike up the costs. So in planning your retirement expenses and the income you will require, you will need to discuss what each person would like to do during retirement. For example, if one wants to travel extensively and the other doesn't, there will obviously be some potential conflicts in retirement expectations. These must be resolved before effective planning can proceed.

If only one spouse is employed, retirement planning will obviously focus on the income of the working spouse. Since you are now living on the income earned by this spouse, you can plan—as you would if you were single—to live on 70 to 80 percent of this income at retirement. Then, like the single person, you will go through the same procedures outlined in the previous scenarios.

But there are a few special concerns that the family in this situation should keep in mind. First, you can expect to receive more Social Security income than you would get if you were single. When you figure your possible Social Security benefits, you should increase the amount of benefits you are projecting by 50 percent. (This assumes that the non-working spouse will be old enough to qualify for Social Security benefits.) For example, a $7,000 annual payment for a single person would be $10,500 for a married couple.[4]

Also, suppose one spouse is covered by a defined benefit pension plan and the other spouse doesn't work or doesn't have a pension. The couple might want to arrange to receive reduced pension payments so that the spouse without the pension can receive a guaranteed pension after the death of the spouse who has qualified for the pension. To facilitate your planning, you will have to find out from your company's human resources department exactly how much this reduced pension payment will be.

One alternative to taking a reduced pension is to provide life insurance for the non-working spouse. If you choose this alternative, though, you will have to lower your retirement income by the amount of the extra life insurance premiums.

If both of you work, you will need to accumulate enough of a retirement nest egg to replace 70 to 80 percent of *both* your incomes. (On the other hand, if you are living on much less than your combined incomes, you should adjust your retirement income goal accordingly.) I usually recommend that when there are two working spouses, each should develop his or her retirement plan independently. One may work longer than the other for a variety of reasons, so do your planning separately and then evaluate the extent to which adjustments should be made to capitalize on the best retirement opportunities available to each of you. For example, only one person may have the opportunity to participate in an employer-sponsored, tax-sheltered savings arrangement.

My son Dan works for an employer that offers a 403(b) plan. His spouse, Sue, is self-employed. At this stage, the best strategy for them seems to be for Sue to reinvest as much as she can afford back into building her business. To make up for what Sue is not putting into savings, Dan has elected to contribute 20 percent of his salary to his 403(b) plan.

A different retirement planning picture has emerged with my son Dave and his wife, Donna. Both are employed by companies that have 401(k) plans, so their main challenge is to decide how much each should put into the respective plans. Some of the factors they have to consider are:

- The percentage of matching contributions each employer is willing to put into the plan. Obviously, there is an advantage to putting more money into the plan which has the highest matching percentage by the employer.
- Vesting rules that determine whether the money contributed by their employer belongs to them if they leave the company. If full vesting occurs after five years of service, and they work only three years, they will lose substantial benefits.
- The attractiveness of the investment options for each plan. They should evaluate the performance of the mutual funds or other investment vehicles in each plan and see which one offers the best record historically and the most flexibility in investment strategy. It won't do any good to choose an aggressive investment strategy for their funds if there is no common stock fund option in the plan.
- Special features of each plan, such as opportunities and penalties for taking out loans or making hardship withdrawals. The more options they can get, the better. An emergency may require them to rely on their 401(k) for a temporary infusion of cash. Although I strongly caution against invading retirement funds, sometimes it's unavoidable.

Perhaps the biggest challenge that marriage presents to the retirement planning process is that spouses have to work together and make key decisions jointly, such as how much each person will save, and how each will invest his or her respective funds. The two of you may have very different levels of risk tolerance. You will need to resolve such differences in order to arrive at a combined plan that suits you both. There may also be a substantial age difference between you. If your spouse is fifteen or twenty years younger and you have young children, a much larger life insurance policy may be appropriate, and you may have to work well beyond age sixty-five.

Now that we've reviewed the four basic retirement planning scenarios, let's try to answer a couple of nagging questions about investment strategy that often remain in the minds of many people: How do I know how much risk I can tolerate? And, How can I become more comfortable with taking reasonable risks?

NOTES
1. See the chart entitled "What You Can Expect Today in Social Security Benefits" on page 197 of the appendix.
2. See the chart entitled "What You Can Expect Today in Social Security Benefits" on page 197 of the appendix.
3. See the chart entitled "What You Can Expect Today in Social Security Benefits" on page 197 of the appendix.
4. See the chart entitled "What You Can Expect Today in Social Security Benefits" on page 197 of the appendix.

CHAPTER FIVE

THE FIVE RULES OF REASONABLE RISK

BUILDING YOUR STRATEGY FOR THE LONG RUN

I am not an investment guru, and I have never pretended to be one. I don't recommend specific stocks, and I won't even endorse a particular mutual fund group—except to advise my clients that they would be wise to stick with the well-established fund organizations that have a proven track record of stability and positive performance over a long period of years.

But even though I'm not a stock-picker and I don't have an investing "system" that promises to make you rich overnight, I do know this: The only way you will succeed in meeting your ultimate investment goals—and retiring comfortably—is to pursue a strategy that involves what I call "reasonable risk."

WHAT IS REASONABLE RISK?

In a nutshell, taking a reasonable risk involves stacking the odds heavily in your favor as you put your money into volatile investments, like common stocks, and hanging in there as your assets fluctuate up and down—sometimes by 10, 20, 30 percent or more.

History offers strong support to those who affirm and follow the reasonable risk-taking philosophy. According to the investment and economics consulting firm Ibbotson Associates, stocks have fared much better during the previous ten, twenty, and thirty-year periods than thirty-day Treasury bills *or* the inflation rate. Here are some comparisons, which go through 1993. The percentages are the compound average annual rates of return for each type of investment.[1]

During the past ten years:
Standard & Poor's 500 stocks (generally larger companies):
   14.9 percent
Smaller Stocks: 10.0 percent
Thirty-day Treasury Bills: 6.4 percent
Inflation Rate: 3.7 percent

During the past twenty years:
Standard & Poor's 500: 12.8 percent
Smaller Stocks: 18.8 percent
Thirty-day Treasury Bills: 7.5 percent
Inflation Rate: 5.9 percent

During the past thirty years:
Standard & Poor's 500: 10.5 percent
Smaller Stocks: 15.0 percent
Thirty-day Treasury Bills: 6.7 percent
Inflation Rate: 5.3 percent

Unfortunately, most people are unreasonably risk-averse when it comes to the stock market. They get rattled when a common stock or growth-oriented mutual fund they own goes down—and there is no escaping the fact that there *will* be dramatic dips in the market.

Wall Street sage Peter Lynch, who managed the huge Fidelity Magellan Fund to tremendous returns during the 1970s and 1980s, noted in a 1995 interview with *Modern Maturity* magazine that fifty stock market declines of 10 percent or more have occurred during the twentieth century. Even more nerve-racking, fifteen of those drops have involved plunges of 25 percent or more in stock prices. That would mean that if the Dow Jones Industrials average was around 4000—as it has been during the writing of this book—the declines would range from 400 to 1000 points!

If he believes the economy is basically healthy, the seasoned investor will literally salivate over one of these drops because they represent fantastic stock-buying opportunities. But more often than not, when one of these dramatic declines occurs in the market, the inexperienced investor falls into a common trap: he sells when his shares are low and sustains serious losses of his principal. Furthermore, after taking a financial bath, the neophyte vows never to "play the stock market" again. Instead, he reverts to slow-growing, "safe" investments, such as bank certificates of deposit or Treasury bills. But as we've seen, these investments aren't safe at all for the long-term investor; rather, they pose a huge risk because they will never provide the return needed over the long term to build adequate funds for retirement.

The only way to avoid this result—and maintain a comfortable income and adequate amount of principal over several decades—is to develop an investment strategy based on "reasonable risk."

To become comfortable with such a strategy, I've found that typically a person must make a commitment to abide by these five fundamental Rules of Reasonable Risk:

Rule 1: Diversify your investments.
Rule 2: Be shrewd in choosing any investment.
Rule 3: Understand the risk of being too conservative.
Rule 4: Work as long as you can.
Rule 5: Start early and be consistent.

Let's examine each of these rules in more depth.

RULE ONE:
DIVERSIFY YOUR INVESTMENTS

Perhaps the most important principle in successful investing is *diversification*. This means, quite simply, that you should spread your money out over a variety of investments so that if one or two go down dramatically, you won't lose everything. Furthermore, you should hold investments in a number of different industries or economic sectors— such as the food industry, autos, utilities, drugs, technology, or foreign businesses. This is just a Wall Street variation on the old saying, "Don't put all your eggs in one basket." Diversification becomes increasingly important in protecting your portfolio as you invest more aggressively—and thus assume more short-term risk.

As a way to understand the power of diversification over a relatively long period of time, compare the experiences of Jim and Katherine. He invested very conservatively without diversifying. She diversified with an extremely aggressive strategy—one that was much more aggressive than what I would recommend for anyone planning for retirement.

Both started out with $5,000. Over a twenty-five-year period, Jim put all of his money into a 5 percent money market account, and at the end of the twenty-five years, he had $16,932.

Katherine, in contrast, chose a *much* more aggressive approach, but spread her risk out over five different investments. Specifically, Katherine put $1,000 into a new business that a local businessman had started—and she lost the entire amount. She put another $1,000 into a small company stock, a new high-tech issue on the over-the-counter exchange, and ended up with no gain—though her $1,000 principal remained intact. A third $1,000, which she invested in the same money market fund as Jim, produced a 5 percent average annual gain—or $3,386—at the end of the twenty-five years. The fourth $1000 was placed in a balanced mutual fund invested primarily in common stocks and bonds. This fund earned 8 percent a year for a total principal of $6,849. Finally, the last $1,000 Katherine placed into a growth stock mutual fund, invested in blue chip common stocks, which earned a 10 percent average annual rate of return—for a value of $10,835.

At an annual average return on her investments of more than 6 percent, Katherine had $22,070—over $5,000 more than Jim—at the end of the twenty-five years, despite her "gun-slinging" approach to investing. If she had followed the moderate or even the less risky aggressive strategy recommended in this book, she would undoubtedly have done even better because she would have minimized the losses on her most speculative investments.

What lessons can we learn about diversification from the experiences of Jim and Katherine? Even though two of the five investment options Katherine chose performed worse than Jim's money market fund, she still came out with a principal that was about 30 percent larger than Jim's, simply because she used a diversified, growth-oriented investment strategy.

Katherine's case is rather extreme because if you invest wisely for retirement—and especially if you do so through an established defined contribution plan—it's highly unlikely that you'll lose all your money. But even in this unusual situation, with an investor who went well *beyond* most definitions of aggressiveness, the protection afforded by diversification helped Katherine achieve a better long-term result than the conservative Jim.

What is the best way for *you* to diversify? One way is to buy individual stocks, but that's not an easy route for any investor—especially those who are new at the game. For one thing, defined contribution programs in most companies offer only mutual funds or similar investments, but not individual stocks. Even if you can invest in individual stocks, to diversify properly you should own shares in at least ten different companies and preferably in at least twenty. This approach requires you to keep on top of the earnings and financial status of each company, just to be sure that it remains economically healthy. You may not even have a large enough sum to diversify adequately in the first place. For example, if you want to own 200 shares each in twenty companies and the cost of a share averages $20, you will have to invest a minimum of $80,000.

Because of such factors, the best bet for most people is to invest in several quality mutual funds. Even with mutual funds, however, wise investing requires careful planning—and that brings us to the second rule of reasonable risk.

RULE TWO:
BE SHREWD IN CHOOSING ANY INVESTMENT

As you may already know, mutual funds are investment firms that manage money. For example, the manager of a growth fund buys stocks in many different companies according to a stated investment philosophy. One fund may specialize in small corporations, another may specialize in large corporations, a third may focus on foreign investments, and a fourth may buy only municipal bonds. The common thread is that mutual funds own a wide variety of different investments—often 100 or more separate companies or holdings. Their *raison d'être* is to allow their investors to profit from the stock market, but to do so under the protection of carefully managed diversification.

Typically, a 401(k) or similar plan will offer at least five options: (1) a common stock fund; (2) a "balanced" fund, which usually has a combination of common stocks and bonds; (3) a fund that keeps the invested principal stable and pays a specified interest rate; such as a money market (4) a fund that invests only in the common stock of your employer's company; and (5) and international fund which invests in securities at non-US companies.

A number of experts predict that in the next decade, the number of fund options in an average 401(k) plan will increase to ten or more— a development that would greatly enhance the investor's ability to achieve an even greater level of diversification.

Even though mutual funds have many advantages, you still have to be careful before you give one of these companies your retirement money. *The Wall Street Journal* recommended in a March 28, 1995 report that in selecting a mutual fund, it's wise to follow these principles:

- Stay away from funds with extremely high annual commissions and expenses. If you pay high "loads" (commissions) and administration fees, you will have that much less to invest.
- Pick an established company that has been around for a while—such as Fidelity Investments; T. Rowe Price; Scudder,

Stevens & Clark; and The Vanguard Group.
- Avoid funds that put all their money into one industry. Remember, you want to *diversify*, and that means spreading your money around among many different industries, including those in foreign countries.
- Stay away from chronically bad performers. If a mutual fund has a good track record, that doesn't mean it will continue to do well in the future. But if the fund has a bad or mediocre track record—especially during periods when other, similar funds seem to be prospering—that is a good sign that you should put your money elsewhere.

How about an index fund?

One increasingly popular way to achieve diversification with mutual funds is to invest in what is known as an "index" fund. These funds buy stocks in all of the companies that are used to determine a particular broad market index, such as the Standard & Poor's 500 index, or the Russell 2000 index. Then, their performance mirrors the movement of the index.

The assumption with this kind of investing is that the broad movement of the market will be up over the long term. Several mutual fund companies now offer funds that are based on various indexes, both in the United States and abroad. But again, in choosing one of these, I would focus on the established mutual fund companies, not on those that have been in operation for only a year or two. Index funds, by the way, have lower investment management fees because the funds are not paying a manager to research and pick the stocks the funds will buy.

RULE THREE:
UNDERSTAND THE RISK OF BEING TOO CONSERVATIVE

A third way to reduce your risk involves a paradox: to lower your risk of ending up with an inadequate nest egg, you must become more aggressive and select more volatile investments.

In our previous discussions of conservative, moderate, and aggressive investment strategies, you have seen that almost everyone should resist the conservative approach and adopt at least a moderate philosophy. Remember, risk is a relative term. In the short-term—say, one to five years—putting your money into fixed income vehicles like certificates of deposit may put you ahead of more speculative, common stock strategies. But as time goes on—typically beyond a ten-year period—the conservative approach steadily loses ground. To reduce your risk of not having enough, resolve to employ either the moderate or aggressive strategy for before-retirement investing, as described in chapter 4.

RULE FOUR:
WORK AS LONG AS YOU CAN

Part of the American dream is to leave the rat race early, but without a doubt, the greatest mistake is to leave *too* early.

During the past decade, companies have been increasing their attempts to cut costs and increase their profits—a trend that has led to what's called "downsizing," or reducing the size of the work force in various companies. About one-fourth of all employers with pension plans offered some sort of early retirement deal between 1991 and 1993, according to the Wyatt Co. consulting firm.

Furthermore, 81 percent of those companies succeeded in convincing their employees to accept these offers, usually by making benefits unusually attractive or loosening eligibility requirements. As a result of these efforts by the nation's corporations, the average retirement age in early 1995 was fifty-eight years, or about two years younger than a decade before. This trend has apparently caught the fancy of younger workers because, as a poll by *Money* magazine in 1993 revealed, 55 percent of all Americans hope to retire before they reach sixty-five. My own consulting has revealed that the typical employee wants to retire by age fifty-five, or even earlier. But some problems have begun to shatter this part of the American dream.

First of all, as we have seen in the previous chapters, early retirement has been placed in jeopardy by the threat of reduced benefits from Social Security and private pensions. There just won't be enough retirement money available to provide a comfortable income for most of those who want to retire before age sixty-five.

Second, people are living much longer today than they did earlier in this century. The current average life expectancy is about seventy-five, in contrast to about forty-seven at the turn of the century. And that's just the *average*. The typical American woman is already living to seventy-nine, and increasing numbers of people live well into their eighties and nineties. In practical, dollars-and-cents terms, this means that your retirement income will probably have to keep pace with inflation over a much longer period of time.

It can be quite sobering to realize that if you retire at age fifty-five, as many younger workers hope to do, and you live to eighty-five, you'll be spending *35 percent of your entire life* not working. Or to put this another way, if you start work at age twenty-one, retire at fifty-five, and die at eighty-five, you will spend almost *half of your adult life* in retirement. This is not what our creator intended. Our lives need to have meaning and purpose.

What Are the Practical Consequences of Early Retirement?
There are several reasons why I advise forgetting early retirement and planning to work longer—reasons that become clear when you consider how the plans of various people worked out in practice.

Marti was widowed when she was fifty-seven years old, and even though she was holding down a satisfying sales job that provided a good income, she elected to quit work. Her husband had left her $150,000 in life insurance benefits, and with the additional $100,000 that she and her husband had accumulated over the years, she figured she could get along nicely. Also, in a few years she expected to file for Social Security benefits, and that would be icing on the cake—or so she supposed.

Unfortunately, at this point—more than twenty years later—Marti has found that her financial expectations don't add up. Thinking she had plenty to "play" with, she took several expensive trips and gave money to her adult children who needed extra cash to purchase homes and start new businesses. As a result, she has ended up with only about $100,000 in principal.

The income from her shrunken investments, her modest Social Security payments, and the impact of twenty years of inflation are making things tight. When an unusual expense comes along, she frequently has to ask one of her children for help. In other words, Marti has gone from an independent retiree to a person who is increasingly dependent on other family members. Her main problem is that she retired early and failed to anticipate how much this premature withdrawal from the work force was going to cost if she lived a normal life span.

Ed worked for the same large corporation for twenty-two years and took an early retirement at age fifty, back in 1977. As he explained, he wanted to "take it easy for a while—I had been working hard all my life." Also, he said he wanted to take a shot at striking out on his own by starting his own consulting firm.

The company had the best of this deal because Ed left well before the main buildup occurred in his defined benefit pension. In fact, he decided to accept a lump sum payment of $40,000—an amount that represented more money than he had ever seen in one check. But this was far less than what the lump sum value of his pension would have been if he had waited until his sixties to retire.

Now only in his late sixties, Ed is already feeling the pinch. He spent all of his retirement money to start his consulting business. Yet even though he has made a modest income, he has failed to earn enough to replace the outlay from his savings or to put anything else aside for retirement. His talents as an entrepreneur just have not been as strong as his ability to work in a large corporation. Now, Ed faces the unappealing prospect of having to keep his consulting business going indefinitely.

Sam had a highly satisfying career as a private preparatory school teacher. He was known as a kind of "Mr. Chips," who nurtured boys and girls through high school and started them out in life with a strong set of personal values and love of learning.

But when he reached age fifty-five, he decided that he would like to take early retirement from his teaching—"because there were so many things I'd taught, but hadn't done in this life. I wanted to travel to Europe, visit museums, attend concerts and operas, and read all the books I'd put aside."

Unfortunately, Sam didn't sit down with a pencil and paper and figure out just how much money he would need to realize his retirement dreams. His school pension and small savings account didn't provide him with enough income to cover much travel. He found he could only afford a few short trips to historical spots near his home, but long vacations to foreign countries were beyond his means.

The most important thing that Sam overlooked was that the greatest fulfillment he had experienced was working with his students and watching them develop into mature, well-educated men and women. After a couple of years, he became bored with his new leisure and began to yearn to return to teaching. But even though he tried to find employment in the academic world, no positions were open for a man his age.

Soon Sam became depressed. He put on weight, seemed to get no joy from his reading—which was the only activity he could afford with any frequency—and four years after his retirement, he suffered his first heart attack. Now, Sam is saddled with heavy medical expenses that have sapped all his savings, and he seems locked permanently into a lifestyle that puts him close to the poverty line.

My purpose in relating these real-life stories is not to depress or frighten you, but to cause you to look very carefully before you leap into early retirement. The experience is rarely quite what you expect. But you can cushion any rough landings you may experience after retirement in one of three ways.

First, if you do retire early—say, in your mid-fifties—one way that you may be able to protect yourself is by accumulating enough money to live well for *at least* another twenty-five to thirty years, regardless of whether or not you work to supplement your retirement income. Obviously, however, saving enough to live on for another thirty or more years without working is a very difficult, if not impossible, trick for most people to accomplish. If you follow the guidelines outlined in this book—and you start early enough—there is some chance you may be able to achieve this feat. But most of us are not in this category.

A second, more viable way for the majority of people to achieve the goal of a comfortable retirement income is to postpone retirement for a few years. You could continue to work at your present job until the maximum retirement age—sixty-five or even older—assuming your employer is willing to keep you on for that long. Or, if you want to keep working but feel there are insuperable problems to doing this in your current job, the best alternative may be to become self-employed—*if* you can manage to make a go of it. I'll discuss my thoughts on starting your own post-retirement business in more detail in chapter 7.

In a *Wall Street Journal* special feature on retirement published on December 9, 1994, the author Lynn Asinof makes a statement that echoes a basic point I have made in this section: "The first step [in planning for retirement] is to stop looking at age sixty-five as a finish line, and focus instead on how long you are likely to live. Then build in lots of flexibility and contingency plans."

Statistics indicate that even today, 50 percent of Americans live beyond age eighty-five, and 10 percent live to age ninety-three. You can expect these numbers to increase in the future—and that puts more pressure on everyone to reduce retirement risks by working to an older age.

Steven Enright, a New Jersey financial planner, sums up the situation when he says that working longer and saving longer "means people don't have to take as much risk. They can sleep better at night."

RULE FIVE:
START EARLY AND BE CONSISTENT

If you start early and put enough money into your investment program regularly, preferably every month or quarter, you will greatly reduce the risks you face in the stock market. There are two reasons for this: the principle of dollar-cost averaging, and the principle of time.

Dollar-Cost Averaging

This proven investment technique involves putting a fixed sum of money into a particular investment—usually a stock or mutual fund—at regular intervals, usually monthly or quarterly. The idea is to invest your predetermined amount *regardless of how the market is doing*.

In many ways, this approach is the opposite of a market-timing investment strategy. With market-timing, you try to buy at those times when the market—and your stock—are low, and you sell when the market is higher. Unfortunately, even the best market-timers may show inconsistent results because determining the uncertain movements of the stock market is akin to making predictions about the future by using a crystal ball.

With dollar-cost averaging, the results are more certain. When the market is down, your money buys more shares of the chosen investment, and when the market is up, it buys fewer. As a result, the investment you end up with over the long haul is *at least* equal to the average price of the up and down markets. But actually, your investment will be worth more than the average if you assume that over a relatively long period of time—at least ten to fifteen years—the overall movement of the market is going to be up.

Suppose you decide to invest $1000 every quarter in a particular fund. The per share price of the fund shares will be different each quarter you invest resulting in the purchase of a different number of shares each quarter. Assume the results are as follows:

Quarter	Amount Invested	Share Value	Number of Shares Purchased
1st	$1000	$10.00	100.00
2nd	1000	9.00	111.11
3rd	1000	10.50	95.24
4th	1000	10.00	100.00
TOTAL	$4,000		406.35

The value after the last purchase would be $4,063.50 (406.35 shares times $10.00), which is $63.50 more than what you have invested. You will have realized a 1.6 percent gain on the total amount you invested even though the share price is the same now as it was when you started to invest.

In other words, in this case, dollar-cost averaging has produced a better result than you would have achieved had you just invested the entire $4,000 at the beginning of the year. You would have purchased 400 shares at $10.00 per share, which would still be worth $4,000.

Another possibility would have been to do what some less sophisticated investors do which is to stop investing when the stock market drops. Because they tend to become cautious when the market declines, such investors would pass up the opportunity to invest when the price is down. Assume in this instance that you did not invest during the second quarter for this reason, and you invested $2,000 during the third quarter instead. Your results would be as follows:

Quarter	Amount Invested	Share Value	Number of Shares Purchased
1st	$1,000	$10.00	100.00
2nd	0	9.50	0.00
3rd	2,000	10.50	190.48
4th	1,000	10.00	100.00
TOTAL	$4,000		390.48

The current value of your shares would be only $3,904.80. You would have lost $158.70 ($4,063.50 minus $3,904.80) because you were afraid to invest during the quarter when the share value dropped.

Long experience by thousands of savvy investors has demonstrated the effectiveness of dollar-cost averaging—and I would highly recommend the approach to you. All it takes is a commitment of a certain amount of money to a particular investment over a relatively long period of time. If you have the discipline to follow through, you will be well on your way to achieving your retirement goals.

Time

To be successful in investing—and to keep your risks to a minimum— you have to give yourself some time. That's why I have emphasized throughout this book how important it is to *start early*. You have to give your investments the opportunity to move through several economic cycles. The more market ups and downs you can negotiate, the more the value of your investment will tend to level out on the upside.

If you have some time before retirement, *use* it by starting your investment strategy right now. Begin immediately with the dollar-cost averaging method, and employ it consistently up until the time you quit work. If you do, you will minimize your risks—and you will be likely to get some of those high returns that were cited in the Ibbotson findings at the beginning of this chapter.

Now let's turn to a final question about retirement planning: How can you get an overall rate of return on your retirement nest egg that will be sufficient to make your financial future secure?

NOTE

1. Source of historical data information on annual returns © *Stocks, Bonds, Bills, and Inflation 1995 Yearbook*™, Ibbotson Associates, Chicago (annually updates work by Roger G. Ibbotson and Rex A. Sinquefield). Used with permission. All rights reserved.

CHAPTER SIX

THE NINE PERCENT SOLUTION
PRINCIPLES FOR ACHIEVING HIGH RETURNS

To be a successful investor, you must develop an "investor's mind," a way of looking at the world that has two essential features.

The first is a reasonable approach to risk, which we discussed in the previous chapter. The second is an expectation that the returns on your investments will average at least 8 to 9 percent per year over the long haul. Without this level of return—which I call the "nine percent solution"—most people cannot achieve their target income for an enjoyable retirement.

Granted, most people don't think in terms of a 9 percent return on their money, either because they are more timid than seasoned investors about taking wise risks, or they assume that a consistent 8 to 9 percent return is well out of their reach. But you must avoid this limited way of thinking if you are to succeed with your retirement goals.

WHY IS A NINE PERCENT GOAL SO IMPORTANT?

It's impossible for most people to keep afloat financially in their later years simply by bringing in a four, five, or even six percent return on their assets. One major reason these lower rates won't work is because of the impact of inflation. Obviously, if you're making only a 4 percent

119

return on your money, and the inflation rate is 3.5 percent, your investments are growing at only a half a percent per year.

The other problem with settling for low rates is that they simply don't deliver the goods over a normal period of retirement preparation. Suppose you manage to save $20,000 and put it into a bank account at 4 percent interest for ten years. Your money will grow to about $29,600 during that period. But if you can push your rate of return up close to 9 percent—say to the 8.6 percent moderate investment strategy rate that we have been using in this book—your $20,000 will be transformed into $45,640 during the same ten-year period. And as time goes on, the gap between the 4 percent rate and the 8.6 percent rate will widen. In twenty years, for example, your original $20,000 will be worth only $43,800 at the 4 percent rate. But at the 8.6 percent rate, you will have $104,140—or a large enough asset base to make a significant contribution to your retirement income.

Because I believe it's essential to achieve a minimum average annual return of between 8 and 9 percent over a relatively long time period, I have stressed the importance of pursuing at least the "moderate" investment strategy before retirement, with an average annual return of 8.6 percent. But even though a return of between 8 and 9 percent is perfectly acceptable for a moderate strategy investor, I have chosen to focus on the upper end of this range—a "nine percent solution"—for two main reasons. First, when you are shooting for a goal, it's easier to think in terms of a whole percentage number rather than a fraction of a percent. Second, I believe in the old maxim that investors, like archers, need to aim above their target in order to hit it. Those who set their sights on 9 percent or more will be most likely to achieve at least the 8.6 percent target that we have set for the moderate strategy.

IS A CONSISTENT NINE PERCENT RETURN REALLY POSSIBLE?

The historical results cited on pages 45-46 show that most prudent investors who are willing to put at least 60 percent of their funds into solid growth stocks can achieve a 9 percent return over long periods of time. These attractive returns almost never can be found in a typical bank savings account because savings accounts don't offer the following components that may go into the returns on stocks and bonds:

Capital Appreciation

The most important component of your average return on common stock will usually be the appreciation in value of the underlying shares. If you buy a mutual fund at $8.00 a share, and the value of the shares rises to $10.00 in the course of one year, you will have a "paper" increase of 25 percent on your money in just that twelve-month period. I use the term "paper" increase because I'm assuming that you won't sell the shares, but will continue to hold them. If you sell the shares, the paper increase becomes a "real" increase, or a capital gain. (If you do sell your shares, by the way, you should immediately make plans to reinvest your gain so you can keep your money working constantly.)

Of course, capital appreciation isn't limited to common stocks. Many people who bought bonds in the mid to late 1980s, for instance, locked in healthy interest rates. Then, they received an additional windfall. When interest rates began to fall in the early 1990s, the underlying price of the bonds soared. (As a general rule, when interest rates go up, the value of bonds decreases; but when rates go down, the value of bonds goes up.) Investors who were watching the movement of the underlying value of their bonds—and not just their interest rates—were able to sell the bonds for profits that at times ranged from 20 to 40 percent of the bonds' face value. However, the value of your bonds would have dropped substantially during 1994 when interest rates increased.

Dividends or Interest

Many stocks—especially the "blue chips" like AT&T or Exxon—pay a regular dividend every quarter, which may average 2 to 3 percent, or even higher. I recommend that before retirement you "reinvest" these dividends by arranging with your stock broker to buy new shares or fractions of shares every time a dividend is paid. The same arrangement can be made with mutual fund companies. After you quit work, you may want to change this arrangement and use the dividends for your retirement income.

An alternative is to accumulate the dividend payments in a separate, liquid retirement account—usually a money market fund. Then, when the fund grows to a certain amount, you can use it to purchase other securities. This way, you achieve a compounding effect—or an exponential growth of your investments that occurs by using your investment income to create additional principal. You plow your dividends back into your assets to buy other stock, which in turn produces other dividends or capital appreciation. In this way, you achieve an "interest-on-interest" compounding effect.

Of course, there are other ways to increase your return through dividends and interest. You might focus on buying relatively stable but high-yielding stocks. Another possibility is to put your money into corporate or government bonds or bond funds, which at the present time can bring you an attractive yield. In certain stages of the economic cycle you may even be able to get very high interest on bank certificates of deposit. But in most periods of history, bank savings accounts haven't come close to the nine percent solution.

These are just a few of the ways that you can put together an investment package that should assure you of an average annual return of 8 to 9 percent, and possibly a lot more. But as you design your investment strategy, you should always be evaluating the return you are getting—and trying to increase your percentage. There are several ways to do this.

PRINCIPLES FOR INCREASING YOUR RETURN

Principle One: Maximize the Compounding Effect

You have already been introduced to the concept of compounding—which has been defined simply as earning interest on interest. The idea is that you put your money into an investment account at a certain rate of interest, but rather than taking the interest out of the account, you add it to your original principal. Thus, future interest is calculated on a larger sum of money. You earn interest on your original principal *plus* the *new* principal created by the accumulation of your interest.

For compounding to work effectively, there are two prerequisites.

Obviously, you must resist the temptation to take the interest out of your account to use it for non-investment purposes. Second, you must give the process as much time to operate as possible.

Table 6-1, which you have used to figure the future value of an investment before retirement, is a good illustration of compounding.

Table 6-1
TABLE FOR PROJECTING CURRENT SAVINGS BEFORE RETIREMENT

Years	**Investment Strategy**		
	Conservative	*Moderate*	*Aggressive*
1	1.062	1.086	1.103
2	1.128	1.179	1.217
3	1.198	1.281	1.342
4	1.272	1.391	1.480
5	1.351	1.511	1.633
6	1.435	1.641	1.801
7	1.524	1.782	1.986
8	1.618	1.935	2.191
9	1.718	2.101	2.416
10	1.825	2.282	2.665
11	1.938	2.478	2.940
12	2.058	2.691	3.243
13	2.186	2.923	3.577
14	2.321	3.174	3.945
15	2.465	3.447	4.351
16	2.618	3.743	4.800
17	2.780	4.065	5.294
18	2.953	4.415	5.839
19	3.136	4.795	6.441
20	3.330	5.207	7.104
21	3.537	5.655	7.836
22	3.756	6.141	8.643
23	3.989	6.669	9.533
24	4.236	7.243	10.515
25	4.499	7.866	11.598
26	4.778	8.542	12.793
27	5.074	9.277	14.110
28	5.389	10.075	15.564
29	5.723	10.941	17.167
30	6.078	11.882	18.935

Each column shows the increase in value of $1.00 at the three different rates of return over a thirty-year period. At the end of year one, the moderate strategy of 8.6 percent leaves you with $1.086. In other words, you earned 8.6 cents on your $1.00 investment. But if you leave that initial $1.00 *plus* the 8.6 cents for a second year at the same rate of return, the total of the interest on the *two* amounts gives you a total of $1.172. And if you follow this procedure for a third year, you end up with $1.281.

In contrast, suppose there is no compounding: you leave the interest you earned in the account, but it just sits there, without entering actively into the process of growth. In that case, your account would still be worth $1.086 the first year. But the next year it would be worth a little less than with compounding—$1.172 instead of $1.179. And the next year, it would be worth still less—$1.258 instead of $1.281. The gap grows larger and larger as the years roll by.

Although the "magic" of compounding is a simple principle, unfortunately far too many people ignore it. Older people may make a good start on setting up a retirement plan, but then invade the principal for something other than a real emergency, which completely undercuts the compounding strategy. Or young people, who can take the greatest advantage of the compounding principle, wait until they are middle-aged to start any serious saving. In fact, according to research done by Stanford University economist B. Douglas Bernheim for Merrill Lynch, the 76 million baby boomers born between 1946 and 1964 are saving only 55.6 percent of what they will need to fund a comfortable retirement beginning at age sixty-five.

If you can avoid these temptations—if you can get started *now* and stick to your strategy—you can be in a strong position to utilize the next principle, which I have called "snowballing."

Principle Two: Take Advantage of Snowballing

"Snowballing" refers to the process of contributing regularly to your investments, even as you achieve a healthy rate of return. In effect, snowballing is an enhanced version of the compounding effect.

For example, suppose you put $1,000 into an IRA account and leave it there for twenty years, at an average annual return of 8 percent—but without making any further contributions from the outside. In twenty years, that account would be worth $4,661—not a bad result, until you compare it with what happens when you "snowball."

To see how this works, suppose that you put in the same $1,000, but then you contribute an additional $100 at the beginning of every year for the next twenty years. At the same 8 percent rate of return, you will end up with $9,137—or nearly twice as much!

A further illustration of this point can be seen in table 6-2. Notice what happens to an investment if you start with $1.00 and then *add* $1.00 every year for a set number of years. As you can see, the results are startling. After twenty years, a moderate investment strategy with this simple technique will yield nearly $49, grown from only a $20 investment.

Table 6-2
TABLE FOR PROJECTING ACCUMULATION OF FUTURE RETIREMENT SAVINGS
BEFORE RETIREMENT

| | **Investment Strategy** | | |
Years	*Conservative*	*Moderate*	*Aggressive*
1	1.000	1.000	1.000
2	2.062	2.086	2.103
3	3.190	3.265	3.320
4	4.388	4.546	4.662
5	5.660	5.937	6.142
6	7.011	7.448	7.774
7	8.445	9.088	9.575
8	9.969	10.870	11.561
9	11.587	12.805	13.752
10	13.305	14.906	16.168
11	15.130	17.188	18.834
12	17.068	19.666	21.774
13	19.126	22.357	25.016
14	21.312	25.280	28.593
15	23.634	28.454	32.538
16	26.099	31.901	36.890
17	28.717	35.645	41.689
18	31.498	39.710	46.983
19	34.450	44.125	52.823
20	37.586	48.920	59.263
21	40.917	54.127	66.367
22	44.454	59.782	74.203
23	48.210	65.923	82.846
24	52.199	72.592	92.379
25	56.435	79.835	102.894
26	60.934	87.701	114.493
27	65.712	96.244	127.285
28	70.786	105.521	141.396
29	76.175	115.595	156.959
30	81.898	126.536	174.126

The above factors are how much $1.00 invested each year will grow to over the applicable number of future years assuming the investment performance for each investment strategy equals historical returns achieved during the period from 1926 through 1993. It has been assumed that the amount you save does not earn any investment income during the year it is invested. This will understate your actual results if you invest the entire amount at the beginning of the year or periodically during the year.

You can achieve a snowballing effect by making a commitment to increase your savings rate each time you get a raise. For example, suppose you are saving 5 percent of your $50,000 salary, or $2,500, and you get a raise to $51,000. If you can put that $1,000 salary increase into your retirement portfolio before you get used to spending the extra money, you will have increased your savings rate by 40 percent!

Principle Three: Work Hard to Reach Your Basic Investment "Blast-Off" Point

It's easy to become distracted or discouraged in the early years of investing because the amounts you accumulate may seem so small. I recall one woman who complained, "I've been putting aside $3,000 a year now for the past ten years, and I've been getting about the 8.6 percent rate of return you recommend. But I still have less than $45,000 to show for it!"

To keep from losing heart, focus on significant intermediate investment goals—including what might be called the "blast-off" point for a powerful investment. This term refers to a certain level of asset value that begins to move you dramatically toward your ultimate retirement goals. Specifically, I have found that there is a point around two times your annual salary where the commitment to a retirement program becomes rock-solid. Also, at this level, excitement begins to build because the finish line is finally in sight.

For example, suppose you earn $40,000 annually and you have managed to pull together a total of $80,000 in retirement funds by age fifty. Also, assume that you are achieving a 9 percent average annual rate of return on your holdings. Now let's suppose you decide you are *not going to put another cent* into this account—but you are going to continue to get the same 9 percent return.

A quick trick for figuring out how a particular asset will do over time at a particular rate is called the "Rule of 72." Someone, somewhere, came up with the insight that if you divide any percentage rate into the number 72, the result or dividend will be approximately the number of years it will take any amount to double at that rate.

Using the rule of 72, you would divide 9 (your rate of return) into 72 to find that your $80,000 will become $160,000 in eight years. Then, in another eight years, your holdings will double again to give you $320,000, by age sixty-six. (Your salary will be around $67,000 at that point if your raises between age fifty and sixty-six average 3.5 percent annually.) This means that if you retired at age sixty-six and dropped your rate of return down to 7.4 percent (the moderate rate of return I recommend *after* retirement), you would generate about $19,950 of inflation-adjusted income ($320,000 divided by 16.04 from Table 7-1). This amount would be sufficient to replace 30 percent of your pre-retirement income.

Of course, you will undoubtedly continue to contribute to your retirement after age fifty, and you'll probably have other sources of income, such as Social Security or a company pension. But the above example is useful to show you that the key to your success remains the blast-off point of at least $80,000 that you achieve at age fifty. For those with higher incomes, a better goal would be to save at least two times your annual income by this point. By reaching that financial threshold, you will manage to put yourself in a position to move up fairly pain-lessly to a nice retirement income.

I know that many of my readers will want to accumulate much more principal than what I'm suggesting, but if you make it to this level, you can be confident that you have broken through an extremely important financial barrier.

Now, we have reached the point where you have all the information and tools you need to do your own retirement planning. So pull out a pad of paper and let's put together a comprehensive personal strategy that will enable you to escape the coming retirement crisis unscathed.

CHAPTER SEVEN

DESIGNING YOUR PERSONAL ESCAPE ROUTE

A STEP-BY-STEP GUIDE

O ne of my main objectives in this book has been to encourage you to consider ways to avoid the traps of complacency and denial that will blindside so many Americans retiring today and in the future. If you are going to be ready for the inevitable crisis that is already beginning to threaten us, you will most likely have to change your lifestyle and your financial habits—and you should act *now* if you hope to maximize your enjoyment and safety after retirement.

To this end, the following pages will help you design your own personal "escape route" from the coming retirement crisis. But before we get to the actual nuts-and-bolts, let's first go through some preplanning steps, which should by now be quite familiar to you.

PREPLANNING STEP ONE:
FIND WAYS TO SAVE MORE MONEY

I've recommended that the minimum amount that most people should be saving is 10 percent of before-tax income. Some may feel that this suggestion is too tough, but in fact, it's a rather modest level of savings, given what some other financial counselors are recommending.

Take the mutual fund maven Sir John Templeton, who founded the

131

phenomenally successful Templeton group of funds, which were recently acquired by the Franklin group. Templeton learned the virtues of thrift when he was growing up in a small Tennessee town. When he graduated from college, moved to New York, and launched his Wall Street career, Templeton made a commitment to set aside 50 percent of his total salary for personal investment. That required plenty of personal sacrifices, such as eating out rarely, cutting corners on furnishings, and never paying more than 16 percent of his "spendable" income for rent. (He defined "spendable" as what was left over after he had paid taxes and put money into his investments.) With this approach Templeton managed to set aside significant amounts of money that he proceeded to invest in the stock market. As a result, he became fabulously wealthy. Now, he lives in a mansion in the Bahamas and funds numerous charitable programs such as the $1 million annual Templeton Prize for Progress in Religion. As you can imagine, he has no trouble making ends meet in retirement.[1]

Templeton's philosophy of savings, which may seem rather radical, actually resonates in one form or another in the popular press. For example, one column in *The Wall Street Journal* published on November 8, 1994, advised that it's possible to save what you need for retirement beginning at age forty-five—as long as you "save like crazy and invest heavily in the stock market."

The writer assumed that you were now earning $50,000 a year and would need $37,000 in inflation-adjusted income at retirement. He suggested that you first push back your targeted retirement age from sixty-five to sixty-seven (sound familiar?). Then, you would assume Social Security payments of $12,000, which would leave you with another $25,000 a year to generate. By setting aside 17.3 percent of your salary each year for the next twenty-two years, and investing 80 percent of your savings in stocks and 20 percent in bonds, you could achieve your goal.

Now, stop for a moment and think seriously about what John Templeton and this *Wall Street Journal* report are saying. You may have thought that I was going overboard with my discussions on savings earlier in this book, but the suggestion of 50 percent savings by Templeton and 17.3 percent by the *Journal* make my recommendations for a 10 percent annual savings rate seem rather modest.

The point is that you should start immediately setting a substantial portion of your income aside. Then, as you get comfortable with investing this much, push the envelope a little. Try to edge those savings upward, to a level that will enable you to reach a truly enjoyable retirement.

PREPLANNING STEP TWO: BE REALISTIC ABOUT SOCIAL SECURITY

What do you think you can actually expect to receive in Social Security income?

First, you should find out from the Social Security Administration exactly where you stand now. Call 1-800-772-1213, and order the required forms to find out your status. This will let you know the amount you will be entitled to if the laws and regulations remain the same up until the time you actually retire. (In the meantime, take a look at the chart entitled "What You Can Expect Today in Social Security Benefits" on page 197 of the appendix.)

How much do you think you can actually count on?

Of course, I don't have a crystal ball, but to be safe, I would suggest that you do your planning with the following guidelines in mind:

- *If you are over sixty:* Assume that your benefits at retirement will be the same as they would be today.
- *If you are fifty to sixty:* Assume that your benefits will be 75 percent of what they would be today.
- *If you are forty to forty-nine:* Assume that your benefits will be half of what they would be today.
- *If you are younger than forty:* Don't count on any benefits at all—or at least no more than 25 percent of what they would be today.

These predictions may seem unduly pessimistic, and I do sincerely hope that I'm proven to be wrong, but I always prefer to be relatively cautious in retirement planning.

PREPLANNING STEP THREE:
IDENTIFY EVERY POSSIBLE SOURCE OF RETIREMENT INCOME

We've already covered this principle in some detail but I want to summarize it here, just so you'll have the relevant issues in mind as you begin your planning. As you are surveying your possible sources of investment income, don't forget:

- *Home equity:* Consider the question of whether or not you should sell your home, or move to a less expensive place.
- *Company pensions:* Keep track of various benefits you may qualify for in the different jobs you have held during your career. They can add up! Also, if your employer provides a defined benefit pension plan, consider staying on this job until the normal retirement age (usually sixty-five). This way, you will get the full benefit of the "back-end loading" referred to in chapter 2.
- *Cash values in whole life insurance policies:* I wouldn't necessarily suggest that you cash these in, either now or immediately upon your retirement. But if you run short of cash as retirement proceeds, the savings component of these policies can provide an often forgotten windfall.

There may be other sources of income that you can think of, such as valuable collectibles like artwork or jewelry. So survey your assets to see if there is anything that might be liquidated and put to work through other investments.

IT'S TIME TO GO TO WORK:
THE RETIREMENT PLANNING WORKSHEETS

The first thing you should do as you begin filling out these forms is to choose the date when you want to retire. If you plan to retire at age sixty-five, go directly to the first worksheet. On the other hand, if you are sure you want to try to retire *before* age sixty-five, you can go to the second worksheet. If you are not sure what date you should pick to quit work, do both of the calculations. That way, you'll have a clear picture of the challenges you are likely to face with either option.

Whatever age you choose for retirement, you will have to use the now-familiar four key tables for retirement planning, which have been reproduced again here to make your planning as convenient as possible. Also, I have included an additional table, table 7-5, "Discounting from Age Sixty-Five to an Earlier Retirement Age." This table will facilitate planning for those who want to retire before age sixty-five.

Table 7-1
AMOUNT NEEDED TO PROVIDE ONE DOLLAR OF
INFLATION-ADJUSTED INCOME AFTER RETIREMENT

Inflation Rate—3.0%			
Investment Strategy	**Number of Years Income Will Be Needed**		
	20	**25**	**30**	**35**
Conservative	$16.08	$19.14	$21.90	$24.38
Moderate	13.36	15.29	16.85	18.12
Aggressive	12.16	13.67	14.82	15.71

Inflation Rate—3.5%			
Investment Strategy	**Number of Years Income Will Be Needed**		
	20	**25**	**30**	**35**
Conservative	$16.78	$20.19	$23.33	$26.23
Moderate	13.91	16.04	17.82	19.30
Aggressive	12.64	14.31	15.62	16.65

Inflation Rate—4.0%			
Investment Strategy	**Number of Years Income Will Be Needed**		
	20	**25**	**30**	**35**
Conservative	$17.53	$21.32	$24.90	$28.25
Moderate	14.47	16.85	18.88	20.61
Aggressive	13.13	14.99	16.48	17.69

Inflation Rate—4.5%			
Investment Strategy	**Number of Years Income Will Be Needed**		
	20	**25**	**30**	**35**
Conservative	$18.32	$22.53	$26.60	$30.54
Moderate	15.08	17.72	20.03	22.04
Aggressive	13.66	15.72	17.42	18.82

Inflation Rate—5.0%			
Investment Strategy	**Number of Years Income Will Be Needed**		
	20	**25**	**30**	**35**
Conservative	$19.16	$23.83	$28.47	$33.05
Moderate	15.71	18.65	21.27	23.62
Aggressive	14.21	16.50	18.43	20.07

Table 7-2
INFLATION ADJUSTMENT TABLE

Number of Years	Assumed Annual Rate of Change				
	3%	3.5%	4%	4.5%	5%
1	1.03	1.035	1.04	1.045	1.05
2	1.06	1.07	1.08	1.09	1.10
3	1.09	1.11	1.12	1.14	1.16
4	1.12	1.15	1.17	1.19	1.22
5	1.16	1.19	1.22	1.25	1.28
6	1.19	1.23	1.27	1.30	1.34
7	1.23	1.27	1.32	1.36	1.41
8	1.27	1.32	1.37	1.42	1.48
9	1.31	1.36	1.42	1.49	1.55
10	1.34	1.41	1.48	1.55	1.63
11	1.38	1.46	1.54	1.62	1.71
12	1.42	1.51	1.60	1.70	1.80
13	1.46	1.56	1.67	1.77	1.89
14	1.51	1.62	1.73	1.85	1.98
15	1.56	1.68	1.80	1.93	2.08
16	1.60	1.74	1.87	2.02	2.18
17	1.65	1.80	1.95	2.11	2.29
18	1.70	1.86	2.02	2.21	2.41
19	1.75	1.93	2.10	2.31	2.53
20	1.80	1.99	2.19	2.41	2.65
21	1.86	2.06	2.28	2.52	2.79
22	1.91	2.13	2.37	2.63	2.93
23	1.97	2.21	2.46	2.75	3.08
24	2.03	2.29	2.56	2.87	3.23
25	2.09	2.37	2.66	3.00	3.39
26	2.15	2.45	2.77	3.14	3.56
27	2.22	2.53	2.88	3.28	3.74
28	2.28	2.62	3.00	3.43	3.92
29	2.35	2.72	3.12	3.58	4.12
30	2.42	2.81	3.24	3.74	4.33

Table 7-3
TABLE FOR PROJECTING CURRENT SAVINGS
BEFORE RETIREMENT

Years	**Investment Strategy**		
	Conservative	*Moderate*	*Aggressive*
1	1.062	1.086	1.103
2	1.128	1.179	1.217
3	1.198	1.281	1.342
4	1.272	1.391	1.480
5	1.351	1.511	1.633
6	1.435	1.641	1.801
7	1.524	1.782	1.986
8	1.618	1.935	2.191
9	1.718	2.101	2.416
10	1.825	2.282	2.665
11	1.938	2.478	2.939
12	2.058	2.691	3.242
13	2.186	2.923	3.576
14	2.321	3.174	3.944
15	2.465	3.447	4.351
16	2.618	3.743	4.799
17	2.780	4.065	5.293
18	2.953	4.415	5.839
19	3.136	4.795	6.440
20	3.330	5.207	7.103
21	3.537	5.655	7.835
22	3.756	6.141	8.642
23	3.989	6.669	9.532
24	4.236	7.243	10.514
25	4.499	7.866	11.597
26	4.778	8.542	12.791
27	5.074	9.277	14.109
28	5.389	10.075	15.562
29	5.723	10.941	17.165
30	6.078	11.882	18.933

Table 7-4

TABLE FOR PROJECTING ACCUMULATION OF FUTURE RETIREMENT SAVINGS BEFORE RETIREMENT

	Investment Strategy		
Years	*Conservative*	*Moderate*	*Aggressive*
1	1.000	1.000	1.000
2	2.062	2.086	2.103
3	3.190	3.265	3.320
4	4.388	4.546	4.662
5	5.660	5.937	6.142
6	7.011	7.448	7.774
7	8.445	9.088	9.575
8	9.969	10.870	11.561
9	11.587	12.805	13.752
10	13.305	14.906	16.168
11	15.130	17.188	18.834
12	17.068	19.666	21.774
13	19.126	22.357	25.016
14	21.312	25.280	28.593
15	23.634	28.454	32.538
16	26.099	31.901	36.890
17	28.717	35.645	41.689
18	31.498	39.710	46.983
19	34.450	44.125	52.823
20	37.586	48.920	59.263
21	40.917	54.127	66.367
22	44.454	59.782	74.203
23	48.210	65.923	82.846
24	52.199	72.592	92.379
25	56.435	79.835	102.894
26	60.934	87.701	114.493
27	65.712	96.244	127.285
28	70.786	105.521	141.396
29	76.175	115.595	156.959
30	81.898	126.536	174.126

The above factors are how much $1.00 invested each year will grow to over the applicable number of future years assuming the investment performance for each investment strategy equals historical returns achieved during the period from 1926 through 1993. It has been assumed that the amount you save does not earn any investment income during the year it is invested. This will understate your actual results if you invest the entire amount at the beginning of the year or periodically during the year.

Table 7-5

DISCOUNTING FROM AGE SIXTY-FIVE TO AN EARLIER RETIREMENT AGE

Number of Years Between Retirement Age and Sixty-Five	Investment Strategy		
	Conservative	Moderate	Aggressive
1	.942	.921	.907
2	.887	.848	.823
3	.836	.781	.746
4	.787	.719	.677
5	.742	.662	.614
6	.699	.610	.557
7	.658	.561	.505
8	.620	.517	.458
9	.584	.476	.415
10	.550	.438	.376
11	.518	.404	.341
12	.488	.372	.310
13	.460	.342	.281
14	.433	.315	.255
15	.408	.290	.231

RETIREMENT PLANNING WORKSHEET ONE:
RETIRING AT AGE SIXTY-FIVE

To determine how large a nest egg you must accumulate to retire at age sixty-five, you should use the worksheet, "Retirement Planning Worksheet one." The first version of this worksheet has already been filled out as an example by an individual who is now fifty years old and is making a salary of $100,000 a year. After you get the feel for how the form works by carefully studying this example, move on to the second version of the worksheet, which is blank. Use the blank form to do your own figuring. (There are pages at the back of this book for you to use for your own financial notes and calculations.) Limited permission is given to copy the worksheets on pages 144 and 149-150 for use in conjunction with this book. No pages in any other part of this book may be copied, nor may the worksheets be copied for any reason other than actual use with this book.

EXAMPLE RETIREMENT PLANNING WORKSHEET ONE
FOR RETIREMENT AT AGE SIXTY-FIVE OR LATER
(COMPLETED BY FIFTY-YEAR-OLD)

1. Your age: 50

2. Your present salary: $100,000

3. Percentage of your salary you would need if you retired tomorrow: 75%

4. Percentage of your salary you expect to receive from Social Security: 10%

5. Percentage of your salary you expect to receive as a monthly pension from an employer-sponsored pension plan: 15%

6. Percentage of your salary that must be provided from other sources (add item 4 and item 5, and subtract the sum from item 3): 50%

7. Number of years you expect to live after age sixty-five: 25 years

8. Investment strategy you expect to follow after retirement (pick one):

   Conservative   (Moderate)   Aggressive

9. Amount you will need for every $1.00 of inflation-adjusted income (use table 7-1 to find the factor that matches the inflation rate you expect, the number of years you expect to live after age sixty-five, and the investment strategy you selected in item 8): 16.04

10. Annual rate at which you expect your personal cost of living to increase between now and age sixty-five (this may be either the rate of inflation you expect, or the annual increase you expect in your own standard of living and expenses): 4%

11. Annual income you would need if you were to retire today (multiply item 2 by item 6): $50,000

12. The size of the nest egg you would need if you retired today (multiply item 11 by item 9): $802,000

13. The size of the nest egg you will need at age sixty-five (multiply item 12 by the factor from table 7-2 that correlates with the number of years you have left until age sixty-five and the cost of living percentage you chose in item 10):

    Factor from table 7-2: 1.80

    Size of nest egg needed at age sixty-five: $1,443,600

14. Amount you have already accumulated for retirement: $300,000

15. Projected value of current savings at age sixty-five (multiply item 14 by the factor from table 7-3 that correlates with your current investment strategy and the number of years that remain before retirement at age sixty-five):

    Factor from table 7-3: 3.447

    Value of current savings at age 65: $1,034,100

16. Amount you must still accumulate between now and age sixty-five (subtract item 12 from item 15): $409,500

17. Annual amount you must save between now and age sixty-five (divide item 16 by the factor from table 7-4 that correlates with your current investment strategy and the number of years remaining until age sixty-five):

Factor from table 7-4: 28.454

Required annual savings: $14,392

18. Percentage of your present salary that must be saved each year (divide item 17 by item 2): 14.4%

The amount you need to save may come either entirely from your contributions, or from a combination of contributions from you and your employer if you have a 401(k) or similar plan.

The above computation also assumes that you will save the same dollar amount each year between now and retirement. So if your salary increases to keep up with the personal cost of living increase indicated in item 10, the percentage of your salary you'll need to save each year will actually decrease.

Finally, if you own your home and expect to sell it when you retire—or if there are other assets you expect to invest to provide income—you should subtract the total value of these extra assets from the amount you need to save in item 16. This, in turn, will reduce the annual savings you will be required to set aside in item 17.

RETIREMENT PLANNING WORKSHEET ONE
FOR RETIREMENT AT AGE SIXTY-FIVE OR LATER

1. Your age:_____

2. Your present salary:_____

3. Percentage of your salary you would need if you retired tomorrow:_____

4. Percentage of your salary you expect to receive from Social Security: _____

5. Percentage of your salary you expect to receive as a monthly pension from an employer sponsored pension plan:_____

6. Percentage of your salary that must be provided from other sources:_____

7. Number of years you expect to live after age sixty-five:_____

8. Investment strategy you expect to follow after retirement (pick one):

    Conservative   Moderate   Aggressive

9. Amount you will need for every $1.00 of inflation-adjusted income:_____

10. Annual rate at which you expect your personal cost of living to increase between now and age sixty-five:_____

11. Annual income you would need if you were to retire today:_____

12. The size of the nest egg you would need if you retired today:_____

13. The size of the nest egg you will need at age sixty-five:_____

14. Amount you have already accumulated for retirement:_____

15. Projected value of current savings at age sixty-five:_____

16. Amount you must accumulate between now and age sixty-five:_____

17. Annual amount you must save between now and age sixty-five:_____

18. Percentage of your present salary that must be saved each year:_____

RETIREMENT PLANNING WORKSHEET TWO: RETIRING PRIOR TO AGE SIXTY-FIVE

If you are like most younger workers I encounter, you are expecting to retire before age sixty-five. If you are middle-aged and haven't done much to prepare for retirement, you have a difficult road ahead of you. But if you start early enough and are sufficiently realistic and disciplined, there is a good chance you will achieve your goal.

I want to emphasize the *early*, *realistic*, and *disciplined* components in this equation. You are going to have to work hard and know exactly where you stand now in order to achieve the demanding objective you have set for yourself.

The first important step will be to fill out the accompanying worksheet 2, which focuses on retirement *before* age sixty-five. As with the previous worksheet, I am first including a form that is already filled out, to help you understand how the calculations work. The assumptions I have made are that the aspiring retiree is now fifty years old, is making $60,000 a year, and expects to retire in ten years, at age sixty.

You'll note that the format of this worksheet is quite different from the one for age sixty-five because several complicating factors are automatically introduced when you begin to think about early retirement. For one thing, you need more money when you retire early because you have to count on fewer working years during which you can save.

Also, I'm assuming that you will receive no Social Security before you turn sixty-five; instead, you will choose to wait so that you can collect your maximum benefits. This means that you have to generate additional income before age sixty-five to make up for the Social Security benefits that won't be available during that period.

As you can see, the illustration I've used, which requires that the person save 69 percent of his or her salary every year, is totally unrealistic. The sample worksheet makes clear several important issues we've already covered: One, the sooner you fill out your own worksheet, the sooner you will find out just how realistic your retirement aspirations are. Two, a conservative investment strategy usually doesn't work.

Three, it's essential to start early, preferably when you have more than ten years to go before you retire. Finally, it's usually not advisable to retire before age sixty-five. This individual has a number of retirement options available, but the one illustrated is certainly not one of them!

EXAMPLE RETIREMENT PLANNING WORKSHEET TWO
FOR RETIREMENT PRIOR TO AGE SIXTY-FIVE
(COMPLETED BY FIFTY-YEAR-OLD)

Nest Egg Needed Beginning at Your Desired Retirement Age, Prior to Age Sixty-Five:

1. Present salary: $60,000

2. Your desired retirement age: 60

3. Number of years between desired retirement age and sixty-five: 5

4. Number of years between now and your desired retirement age: 10

5. Annual rate at which you expect your personal cost of living to increase between now and your desired retirement date (this figure may be the projected inflation rate, or the annual increase you expect in your expenses and standard of living): 3%

6. Your projected salary at retirement (multiply item 1 by the factor from table 7-2 that correlates with the number of years remaining before your retirement date from item 4, and your projected annual cost of living increase from item 5):

    Factor from table 7-2: 1.34

    Projected salary at retirement: $80,400

7. Early retirement nest egg needed (multiply item 3 times item 6): $402,000

Nest Egg Needed at Age Sixty-Five:

8. Percentage of your salary you would need if you retired tomorrow: 75%

9. Percentage of your salary you expect to receive from Social Security: 30%

10. Percentage of your salary you expect to receive as a monthly pension from an employer-sponsored pension plan: 15%

11. Percentage of your salary that must be provided from other sources (add item 9 and item 10, and subtract the sum from item 8): 30%

12. Number of years you expect to live after age sixty-five: 20

13. Investment strategy you expect to follow after retirement (pick one):

    (Conservative)   Moderate   Aggressive

14. Amount you will need for every $1.00 of inflation-adjusted income (find the factor on table 7-1 that correlates with the number of years you expect to live after age sixty-five from item 12, and the investment strategy you selected in item 13): 16.08

15. Income you would need if you were to retire today (multiply item 1 by item 11): $18,000

16. Size of the nest egg you would need to generate the income in item 15 if you retired today (multiply item 14 by item 15): $289,440

17. Size of the nest egg you will need at age sixty-five to generate the income in item 15 in today's inflation-adjusted dollars (multiply item 16 by the factor from table 7-2 that correlates with the number of years remaining until you reach sixty-five and the percentage you chose for item 5):

    Factor from table 7-2: 1.56

    Size of nest egg needed at age sixty-five: $451,526

18. Amount you will need by your desired retirement age (multiply item 17 by the factor from table 7-5 that correlates with the investment strategy you expect to follow after retirement and the number of years you chose in item 3):

    Factor from table 7-5: 0.740

    Amount you will need by your desired retirement age: $334,130

Total Nest Egg You Will Need When You Retire Early:

19. Add item 7 and item 18: $736,130

20. Amount you already have accumulated for retirement: $120,000

21. Projected value of current savings at your expected retirement age (multiply item 20 by the factor from table 7-3 that correlates with your current investment strategy and the number of years you chose in item 4):

    Factor from table 7-3: 1.825

    Projected value of current savings at retirement: $219,000

22. Amount you still have to save before your desired retirement (subtract item 21 from item 19): $517,130

23. Annual savings required between now and your desired retirement age (divide item 22 by the factor from table 7-4 that correlates with your current investment strategy and the number of years remaining until your expected retirement):

    Factor from table 7-4: 13.305

    Annual amount you must save: $38,867

24. Percentage of your salary that must be saved each year, from now until your desired retirement date (divide item 23 by item 1): 65%

RETIREMENT PLANNING WORKSHEET TWO
FOR RETIREMENT PRIOR TO AGE SIXTY-FIVE

Nest Egg Needed Beginning at Your Desired Retirement Age, Prior to Age Sixty-Five:

1. Present salary:_____

2. Your desired retirement age:_____

3. Number of years between desired retirement age and sixty-five:_____

4. Number of years between now and your desired retirement age:_____

5. Annual rate at which you expect your personal cost of living to increase between now and your desired retirement date:_____

6. Your projected salary at retirement:_____

7. Early retirement nest egg needed (multiply item 3 times item 6):_____

Nest Egg Needed at Age Sixty-Five:

8. Percentage of your salary you would need if you retired tomorrow:_____

9. Percentage of your salary you expect to receive from Social Security:_____

10. Percentage of your salary you expect to receive as a monthly pension from an employer-sponsored pension plan:_____

11. Percentage of your salary that must be provided from other sources:_____

12. Number of years you expect to live after age sixty-five:_____

13. Investment strategy you expect to follow after retirement (pick one):

   Conservative   Moderate   Aggressive

14. Amount you will need for every $1.00 of inflation-adjusted income:_____

15. Income you would need if you were to retire today:_____

16. Size of the nest egg you would need to generate the income in item 15 if you retired today:_____

17. Size of the nest egg you will need at age sixty-five to generate the income in item 15 in today's inflation-adjusted dollars:_____

18. Amount you will need by your desired retirement age:_____

Total Nest Egg You Will Need When You Retire Early:

19. Add item 17 and item 18:_____

20. The amount you already have accumulated for retirement:_____

21. Projected value of current savings at your expected retirement age:_____

22. Amount you still have to save before your desired retirement:_____

23. Annual savings required between now and your desired retirement age:_____

24. Percentage of your salary that must be saved each year, from now until your desired retirement date:_____

Now you should have a handle on the personal retirement program that makes the most sense for you. If you're considering continuing to earn income after your official retirement date, your options will be even broader. Many retirees choose to start their own businesses after they leave the traditional work force. But succeeding as an entrepreneur isn't easy. This kind of transition requires considerable planning and significant skills that most workers don't develop while employed at a large company. To put it bluntly, if you try to start your own business *after* you quit, without accumulating some experience beforehand, you may find yourself in big financial trouble.

SHOULD YOU LAUNCH A NEW BUSINESS AFTER YOU RETIRE?

The American Association of Retired Persons has estimated that one-fifth of its members have serious plans to start their own business or work for themselves. But a survey reported on February 14, 1995 in *The Wall Street Journal* showed that there are often many obstacles along the way.

For example, the *Journal* study cited the experience of one fifty-nine-year-old engineer who left his high-paying job with a large corporation to start his own software company. Unfortunately, this man lost about $300,000 of his money on the effort, and at age sixty-five, he found himself doing extra consulting work to pay off the debt.

There are many problems that may emerge when a worker from a relatively large company—even a worker with considerable management experience—tries to start up his or her own enterprise. For example, the inexperienced entrepreneur may overstaff his fledgling company—mainly because that was the way that his old company was staffed. Or he may lack the skills in managing cash flow in a small operation. Or he may not have some key training, such as a knowledge of how to market his product or services.

It's estimated that one out of every five new businesses fails in the first five years of operation. That's simply not a risk that most retirees can afford to take lightly. It's essential to go to great lengths to prepare yourself to succeed in any new venture you undertake late in life.

But having issued all these grave warnings and enumerated all the things that can go wrong with a start-up business, let me say this: I believe that starting your own business is often the best approach to take as you near retirement. This is especially true if you are in a company where it won't be possible for you to work until your early sixties and then take advantage of a good pension program.

At a minimum, before you launch your own business, you should be certain to:

- Delay leaving your present company for as long as you can, and when you do decide to leave, negotiate hard to obtain the best severance package you can. Try not to settle for an amount that will leave you seriously strapped for funds in the first few years after you cut the ties.
- Start your new business as early as possible, preferably several years before you quit your present job. If possible, there should be an overlap between your new job and the one you're leaving so that you'll be able to maintain a steady stream of income as you get your feet on the ground in the new venture.
- Do a thorough job of educating and preparing yourself for your new position. Be sure you really understand what it means to run a small, independent business.

One surprise for some newly self-employed people is that you need to plan on doing everything yourself, regardless of how demanding the task. Often, you can get good advice and guidance from local organizations formed by volunteer retirees who have been successful in starting and running their own businesses. Check with your local Chamber of Commerce. Also, you may be able to get help from your local chapter of the National Association of the Self-Employed (NASE), which has national headquarters at 2121 Precinct Line Road, Hurst, TX 76054 (1-800-827-9990).

Despite the effort and time that it takes, I'm a great believer in shifting over to a self-employed status as you near traditional retirement age—and I feel this way for some very personal reasons. You see, a number of years ago, I made a commitment to the very route that I'm suggesting you take—though admittedly, I have made my share of mistakes along the way.

A PERSONAL JOURNEY TOWARD RETIREMENT

I spent most of my working life as an owner-consultant in my own benefits consulting firm. My partners and I started the business from scratch, built it into a company of over 300 employees, and sold it during 1990 when I was forty-eight years old.

When the new company terminated me at the end of my contract with them at age fifty-one, I had a major decision to make. I could really "retire," in the sense that I would just quit work. Or I could begin a job search, hoping that I would be able to secure a position with a major consulting firm or a large financial organization. Or I could start over on my own.

I decided that I didn't want to retire. For one thing, I was afraid of getting bored and not being able to do something useful during my older years. Also, as a retirement specialist, I was more aware than most people of the dangers of quitting work too early. I had encountered more than one situation where a person would live for several decades and gradually see his income squeezed more and more by the steadily increasing cost of living.

Because I was in good health and wanted to stay active, it seemed wise to consider taking out a kind of "insurance policy" in the form of starting my own business to increase my later retirement income. But before I made a final decision, I did some serious soul-searching.

As I considered my alternatives, God made me aware that he had given me a clean slate, and that meant I had an opportunity to do something entirely new with my life. Many times during my career I had assumed new responsibilities because it had seemed best for the company or for the other employees. Now, I began to ponder and pray about what would be the best thing for *me* at this stage of my life. As I mulled things over, I created this "wish list":

- A number of nonprofit organizations and ministries were at the top of my list of priorities. Yet I wanted to devote my time to them without the tension of having to justify my activities to some outside employer or company.
- I wanted to do something that would be of significant value to my clients, whoever they might turn out to be.
- I wanted to do something I enjoyed.
- I did not want to have to set any time limits on the age at which I would stop working. I wanted the option to continue up until age sixty-five or beyond.
- I wanted to have the freedom to work in any geographical area.
- I wanted to be able to provide financial assistance, if the need arose, to my four grown children.

After I completed this list, it became clear that I wasn't likely to be able to achieve my goals by seeking employment with another big company. So I decided to start over on my own—with the expectation that it would take me three years to get back to the income I had earned during 1993.

Certainly, it would have been easier and probably less stressful, at least initially, for me to become an employee of some big organization. But I knew if I chose that route, I probably wouldn't survive for more than five years in a new, highly political corporate environment.

Furthermore, I had some confidence in my ability to make it on my own because I had been heavily involved in marketing and sales during all of my years as a consultant. As a result, the idea of having to develop a new business from the ground up—and sell my services to the public—didn't seem overwhelming. In general, I find it is more difficult for individuals who have never had to initiate business to start their own operation successfully.

As is the case with most people blazing the trail of self-employment, my path to my present position hasn't always been easy. Above all, I have had to be very careful to preserve my assets, including my *own* 401(k) funds, some business real estate, and the equity in our home. This has meant adjusting our standard of living for a while so that I could cut expenses and make more money available for the business. I have also been blessed by a very supportive wife, who has been a great source of encouragement in my new venture.

Some people might not be quite as cautious as I have been in protecting their assets. But I'm all too aware of the many unexpected things that can go wrong when you are starting up a new business and trying to lay a solid foundation for retirement at the same time. You can *hope* that your expectations for producing income from your new venture will bear fruit, but just to be safe, it's wise to protect your capital so that you'll have enough financial backup in case unpleasant surprises occur.

It's fortunate that I took this approach because, predictably, some of my ideas for generating income did not work out as I had planned. For one thing, I wanted to plunge into providing a series of retirement seminars. But that venture didn't succeed as well as my decision to establish the 401(k) Association, a lobbying and advocacy organization for plan participants and sponsors. Also, some public speaking and publishing efforts, including a newsletter for the Association, have produced much better results. Now, the rough transition period for establishing a new business seems mostly behind me, and the way appears open to build on my successes. I may even return to some of my original ideas, such as the seminar offerings. But more than anything else, I'm thankful that I won't be forced to retire earlier than necessary just because some boss or corporation has elected to push me out.

But I'm just one example of how a transition can be made to an end-of-career job that doesn't mandate some unpalatable form of early retirement. We can also derive some important lessons from others—including a cable television executive who relied on some unique foresight and planning to design his own "unending career" scenario.

A LESSON FROM A CABLE TV ENTREPRENEUR

When he was in his mid-forties, "success panic" struck Bob Buford, a highly successful Texas cable television company owner who had extended his business into a multi-million-dollar mini-empire that spanned eight states. Buford had all he wanted in the way of worldly goods, and he could easily have decided to stop work and head for a Caribbean Island for a few years.

But as he relates in his book *Halftime* (Zondervan, 1994), Buford did not want to quit work, and he wasn't interested in continuing on his track of accumulating more and more money and business power. Instead, he had begun to ask himself the question, "How much is enough?" His answer: he already had enough—and now he had to decide what to do with the rest of his life.

Granted, Buford was different from most of us in that he wasn't confronted with the problem of how to accumulate enough money for retirement. He had already done that many times over. But he was facing a very difficult question that most of us *do* have to answer: Do I want to retire early, or will my life be more meaningful if I continue to work?

His answer was that during the "second half" of his life, he did want to continue to work—but not on the terms he had chosen in the past. One difference was that he wanted his new work to count for something more than profit-making. Also, he wanted to continue to pursue his new interests well into the future, without having to fear being terminated after some arbitrary number of years. As Buford researched how he might achieve his goal, he discovered a number of truths and principles that you should also find helpful as you try to organize the last part of your life.

First of all, he didn't just drop his old business and immediately start looking for something else to do. He concluded that that would have been unwise and precipitous. Instead, he continued with his old job as president of his company, but at the same time, he began to put out probes to do some occupational "seismic testing." This involved talking with trusted advisers or finding experts he felt could increase his knowledge and provide him with guidance in finding the fresh direction he was seeking.

Buford's objective was to determine just what positions or possibilities might be available, and how he might best be able to use his talents and financial resources to serve others during the second half of his life. But this was no easy assignment. Many people had conducted such a search for their entire lives without finding meaningful answers. So he knew it was essential to be thorough and deliberate as he gathered information and made his decisions.

Finally, after extensive investigation, Buford concluded that he should continue to spend a relatively small portion of his time, about 20 percent, with his television company. This would provide continuity and give him a platform to pursue his main interest—forming an organization called "Leadership Network," which would serve as a support network for leaders of large churches.

After making his decision to launch this new venture, Buford followed a principle articulated by his mentor, the management guru Peter Drucker. Buford paraphrases Drucker's conclusions this way:

> [R]etirees have not proved to be the fertile source of volunteer effort we once thought they would be. They cut their engines off and lose their edge. Peter believes that if you do not have a second or parallel career in service by age forty-five, and if you are not vigorously involved in it by age fifty-five, it will never happen.[2]

When you encounter him in person, you can't help but note that Buford is a man who is quietly confident about the radical decision he made in middle age to change careers. Whatever uncertainties and second thoughts he may have harbored as he was making his transition—and there were a number of them when he was conducting his "seismic testing"—have long since departed. Now, personal satisfaction and a deep sense of mission have gripped him. He is clearly committed to his present course for the foreseeable future, if not for the rest of his life.

Although there is plenty to be learned from such experiences, perhaps the most useful insights we should take away are these:

- Take time to evaluate what values or interests are really most important to you, and how you can best promote or pursue those values in a final career move. You're much more likely to show staying power and to enjoy high energy levels well into your later years if you can truly get excited and involved in your new work.

- Do some hard research into how viable your new career idea is. Is there really a good chance of success? How much will it cost? What do you stand to lose if the venture fails?

- Focus on serving the needs of others. During my years as an employee benefit consultant, I provided advice to many different clients, ranging from small family owned businesses to large, publicly owned companies. Those that were successful had one thing in common: a purpose other than making money. My clients that were interested solely in making money usually consistently missed the mark. The most successful clients were ones where the chief executive had a clear vision of the purpose and mission of the business beyond making a profit. It is likely to be a big mistake for you to venture into your own business without a clear purpose and mission that includes helping others.

- When you finally settle on your pre-retirement career, begin pursuing it simultaneously with your current job. That is, in the sense that Peter Drucker talked about, develop a concept of "parallel careers," so that the transition from one to the other will be smoother. If you quit one job without laying groundwork for the next entrepreneurial venture, you will greatly reduce your chances of succeeding in the second job.

Now, in practical terms, how exactly do you go about preparing yourself for this "final career," which will continue indefinitely? I've discovered several basic guidelines, which, if followed, should greatly increase your chances of succeeding in an independent venture late in life.

HOW TO BEGIN YOUR INDEPENDENT ENTERPRISE

This is not primarily a book about how to start a new business and succeed at it when you are fifty-plus. Still, I do want to share a few powerful, practical principles that I've learned from my clients, as well as from my own personal experiences. These principles should get you off to a strong start no matter how old you are.

Principle one: Do not use your retirement savings to start your parallel career or to cover your living expenses. Instead, use money you earn from your present job, severance pay you receive, or other savings, such as home equity. Stay at your present job long enough to achieve these goals, even if you don't like what you are doing.

Principle two: Do not touch your retirement fund. You will need this money later to live on if your new career doesn't succeed. Remember, one of the main reasons you have decided to keep working is to postpone the need to invade your retirement funds. If you have to dip into your retirement assets to cover daily expenses, those funds will shrink rather than grow. Such a course will place you in danger of eventually having to obtain any available employment you can find in order to survive.

Principle three: Adjust your standard of living to fit your new situation. Eliminate all non-essential expenditures. You cannot afford to continue spending as though nothing has changed. Also, keep your business expenses for the new venture as low as possible. It's easier to adjust for unexpected favorable results than for the reverse. One of the biggest mistakes new business owners make is to overestimate expected income and to underestimate expected costs.

Principle four: Learn how to market yourself. Become proficient in the art of selling the services or products that will bring in the minimum income you have decided you need to avoid invading your retirement funds. Unless you have had some background in direct sales and marketing—and that means face-to-face dealings with prospective clients and buyers—I would suggest you acquire some training in this area.

Unlike the situation in a larger company, you'll find yourself having to wear many hats when you begin your independent venture. Perhaps the most important of these is *selling the product or services* that will be bringing in your income. I've met many people who simply don't know how to persuade another person to buy their services. They may be vague or unclear in their initial sales presentation. Or they do a fine job of explaining their product or service—but then they either forget or become timid about closing the sale. The number-one reason for lost sales is the fact that the customer is never asked to buy the product or service. Yet even the most inexperienced professional salesman knows that to finish off a sales presentation, you have to ask a direct question that calls for a commitment. For example, you might say something like this: "Do you want to buy now?" Or "Do you want to sign up now?" Or "Would you like me to send you a contract so that we can get started on this project?"

A failure to close a sale properly, present yourself effectively, or otherwise do a good marketing job can be overcome by taking a course in selling or even buying a book on the subject and then putting what you learn into practice. Whatever approach you choose, one thing is certain: If you can't market yourself, your services or product, you won't get to first base in generating the money you need to support yourself in your later years.

Principle five: Do some networking. Every corporate outplacing service will tell you that the key to being rehired after you have lost your job is to ask for help or references from all the people you know—and the more you know the better. The same rule applies to starting up a new business. And the younger you are when you begin to build potential business contacts, the better.

Still, it's never too late for networking. I wasn't great at networking myself, and as a result, my new business was slower getting started than it might have been. Yet gradually over the years, I've drawn inspiration from others, including one fifty-four-year-old woman who decided she was tired of her job as a banker, but who couldn't afford to retire early because she hadn't built up enough value in her pension plan. Also, she didn't want to stop working because she still felt she could make some contributions to society in ways that could reach well beyond the realms of commerce and industry.

In particular, she wanted to develop a business giving financial advice to nonprofit organizations. So she proceeded to formulate a business plan and "crunch some numbers" to project potential profits and losses for her new undertaking. This way, she felt she would have a better idea of the kind of living she could realistically expect from the business.

As part of her preparation, she formulated what she called her "list of 100," or the 100 top people she knew who might be able to help her in her new venture. Then, she actually set up a schedule for calling each of these people over a five week period—four people a day, five days a week.

As might be expected, the large majority of her contacts couldn't give her any immediate help. But sixteen of the people she called—an impressive 16 percent of her contacts—gave her additional leads or tentatively promised to give her business when she finally got started. As a result of less than one year of such preparation, this woman was able to quit her job with the bank and to embark almost immediately on a profitable new career.

Principle six: Increase your visibility in the community where you plan to start your venture. With many new businesses, such as those involving personal services, it often doesn't take many clients to produce a nice initial cash flow. So after you've exhausted your personal contacts—including a "list of 100"—you should take other steps to increase your visibility in the community and to stimulate the general public's awareness of what you are offering.

One way to do this is to join community service and social organizations, like the Kiwanis or Junior League, and talk up your new venture among the membership. Also, many office buildings and neighborhood associations have free directories and listings that they compile to communicate the nature and location of different business opportunities. Another possibility is to run inexpensive ads in the local newspaper. A small space ad or classified notice costs very little and may bring in a few clients. An even more effective approach is to come up with a newsworthy angle on your new venture.

One worthwhile question to ask yourself is this: "Is there something about my business that could add some cultural benefits to the community?" For example, if you are planning to offer services to help local nonprofit organizations or government agencies, editors might think your efforts would be worth an article. They are predisposed to promote movements or organizations that seem to enhance the good of their community. And if you are advertising regularly in your local newspaper, the paper will often be more favorably disposed to running an article on your venture. With newspapers in small cities or towns, editors are particularly sensitive to keeping their advertisers happy—and an occasional "freebie" article is sometimes considered a good way to accomplish this. As a general rule, by the way, regular articles have more impact and generate a better response than paid ads. In part, this is because news stories are read more than ads, and in part it's because news stories are assumed by readers to be more objective—and thus more true—than the advertisements.

As I've said, this book isn't intended to answer all your questions about how to start up your own business or to equip you completely to work happily past age sixty-five. But some of these principles and guidelines should at least point you in the right direction.

Of course, it may be that you'll be able to stay on at your present job after you pass sixty-five. If that is possible, you could have the best of all worlds: You may be able to increase the size of your eventual retirement benefits *and* avoid the headaches and start-up costs associated with shifting from a regular job to self-employment.

For example, I would advise anyone who has a 401(k), who can continue to work at a satisfying job up to age seventy, and who can keep contributing to the plan, to do so. That extra five years of contributions and investment growth, from age sixty-five to seventy, can make a huge difference in the final payoff. But for most of us, our employers or circumstances start increasing the pressure to retire much earlier than this. So if you are in your late forties to mid-fifties, I would suggest that you forget any fifty-five retirement fantasy you may be harboring. Instead, begin to think seriously about developing a "parallel career," and work as long as you possibly can. With this approach, you will have some good protection—regardless of what happens in the outside world or what your employer decides to do.

NOTES
1. William Proctor, *The Templeton Touch* (Garden City, NY: Doubleday, 1983), pp. 50-52.
2. Bob Buford, *Halftime* (Grand Rapids, MI: Zondervan, 1994), p. 111.

CHAPTER EIGHT

STAYING PROACTIVE

WHAT YOU CAN DO TO PROTECT
YOUR RETIREMENT RIGHTS

T he most important message I want to get across is that even though we Americans are facing a retirement crisis, you have the ability to protect yourself and achieve a comfortable, enjoyable life after your working years are finished.

But there is also another message—which may be just as important as the first: You have the power to contribute significantly to the preservation of the private and public pension systems in this country. All it takes is a reasonable plan of activism and a willingness to do what it takes to put that plan into effect.

There was a time when I assumed, like most people, that even though I lived in a democracy, my voice alone didn't make much of a difference. In the past decade, I have come to understand just how mistaken I was. In fact, I learned through a series of adventures in the strange world of government regulation that sometimes one person can make a difference—a *huge* difference—if he or she just picks a worthy issue and is persistent in promoting it.

A PERSONAL ADVENTURE WITH GOVERNMENT
RETIREMENT REGULATION

While I was doing some research for a client at the small employee benefits consulting firm where I worked in the fall of 1980, section 401(k), a new passage in the Internal Revenue Code caught my attention. This particular section had been added to the Code by the Tax Revenue Act of 1978. It was an effort by legislators to resolve a conflict between Congress and the Treasury Department over a particular type of profit-sharing plan that was common among major banks.

These banks had set up profit-sharing arrangements where a certain amount of money was contributed by the employer to a retirement fund established for the eligible employees. Each employee had a choice: He could have all of the money put into the tax-deferred retirement fund and thus avoid being taxed on the whole amount. Or he could take part of the money immediately as a taxable cash distribution, with the rest going into the retirement fund.

Predictably, the fact that most higher-paid employees elected to put the entire amount into the plan to delay paying taxes—while most lower-paid employees took as much cash as possible—raised a big red flag with the tax collectors. They were especially troubled by the fact that higher-paid people were getting most of the tax breaks. The Feds said they were "studying" the viability of the tax-deferred nature of the contributions—a threatening stance that threw this type of retirement plan into uncertainty.

When Congress had passed the Employee Retirement Income Act during 1974, a provision had been included prohibiting the Treasury from taking further action with respect to these plans. But, the cloud of uncertainty surrounding these plans continued. Finally Congress resolved the matter by adding Section 401(k) to the Code when the Revenue Act of 1978 was passed. This small addition to the Code provided for the continuation of these plans by adding a non-discrimination test they must meet each year. The initial test limited the amount the highest-paid one-third of the participants could put into the plan to the average amount that the lowest paid two-thirds put in, plus an acceptable spread between the two average percentages. This new provision of the law became effective on January 1, 1980.

There are several points that are of political significance that should be noted at this point:

- January 1, 1980 passed as an uneventful day. There wasn't any mad rush to establish 401(k) plans because this section was added to the Code merely to deal with a special type of profit sharing plan.
- The expected revenue loss when 401(k) was added to the Code was only a few million dollars, again because the provision was expected to have only limited impact.
- Despite the fact that now over 25 million workers are covered by 401(k) plans, these plans do not have any political champion. There wasn't nor has there ever been a presidential candidate or member of Congress who has embraced these plans. The programs do not exist because some politician thought it would be a great idea to establish such a plan to help American workers save for retirement.

In the fall of 1980, while I was on an assignment with a client bank, I began to ponder 401(k) again. The bank officials were interested in revamping their retirement and cash bonus programs because they felt they were at a disadvantage with their competitors. They suggested dropping the cash bonus plan and replacing it with a deferred profit-sharing arrangement in which the entire amount of money would be put into the plan for retirement. I cautioned them against this step, however. I knew from my past experience that most lower-paid employees wouldn't be happy about losing the ready money that they were getting through a cash bonus.

Enter the 401(k) retirement savings plan. Using this provision of the Code, I proposed that we could legally set up the kind of program the bank wanted. But there was a potential snag. To satisfy the 401(k) section, many of the lower-paid employees would have to *choose* to put their money into the retirement plan. The 401(k) provision required a balance between the contributions of the lowest- and highest-paid employees.

But how could you get the lower-paid workers to give up cash in hand and put their money into a retirement fund, with the payoff postponed until the dim and distant future? Clearly, the lower-paid workers needed a strong incentive to participate. So, I proposed that the employer *match* the employee's contribution by putting in extra money.

Here's the illustration I used in presenting this strategy to the bank:

Assume that an employee makes a $1000 contribution to the plan. This would immediately result in a tax savings—of say $200. Also, the employer would put in a matching contribution—of let's say 25 percent of the employee's contribution, or $250. This was an amount of money that the worker wouldn't receive unless he participated in the plan.

It was my hope that the combined incentive of tax savings ($200) plus matching money from the bank ($250) would add up to such an attractive sum (a total incentive of $450) that most employees couldn't ignore it. In this way, the 401(k) provision could be used to benefit *both* the average, lower-paid workers and the higher-paid employees who couldn't establish the plan unless the lower-paid people participated. Unfortunately, the bank I was dealing with decided not to implement my plan because they felt it was too likely to be challenged by the IRS. Our consulting firm tried to sell the 401(k) concept to a couple of large insurance companies, but we were turned down across the board.

Still convinced the concept had merit, we decided to implement the 401(k) plan on our own—and we chose our own firm as the first guinea pig. We, like many other employers, had an after-tax thrift or savings plan. Employees could make after-tax contributions to the plan, and our company matched the employee contributions at a rate of 25, 35, or 50 cents per dollar, depending upon the employee's years of service. We converted this plan to a 401(k) pre-tax savings plan—which became operational on January 1, 1981. This program made history as the first 401(k) retirement savings plan in the country. Now, employees could reduce their salaries by making pre-tax contributions before they received a matching employer contribution.

Of course, neither the matching contribution nor the salary reduction concept was specifically mentioned in the law. But in dealing with the Internal Revenue Code over the years, my approach has always been that unless the law tells me something isn't possible, I assume it *is* possible.

People who know me well know that I was not smart enough to come up with these ideas on my own, and they are correct. I was in fact given these ideas in response to prayer. It is my practice to seek heavenly advice whenever I am facing a major challenge. In this instance, I had become frustrated because most of my business career to that point had involved designing retirement plans for small business owners and professionals. These programs provided the largest possible tax break for the top people, and typically the smallest possible benefit for the lower-paid employees. This type of consulting had lost its appeal because those who were getting most of the benefits needed them the least. Therefore, I had been praying for some time for an opportunity to do something more rewarding. I'm convinced that God directed me to 401(k) in response to that search.

I was so excited about this new concept that I wanted to begin aggressive marketing of the 401(k) plan immediately on a wide scale, but my partner was more cautious. He was concerned about what the federal government might do when they realized how much revenue they were about to lose. After all, we had established a model for literally millions of workers to reduce their taxable income and put increasing amounts of their money—not to mention their employer's matching funds—into tax-deferred retirement accounts. So my partner insisted that we check with some contacts of his in the Reagan administration, just to be sure that our strategy was on firm footing.

We had a meeting with Drew Lewis, then the Secretary of Transportation, and also with Congressman Jack Kemp. I told Kemp that the IRA program that was being expanded then wasn't necessary because the 401(k) plan was already on the books. Also, wanting to be completely up front, I warned him that within a couple of years, the 401(k) plans would result in the loss of $4 to $5 billion per year in tax revenues.

I had expected a warm welcome because increasing savings and capital formation was a major part of President Reagan's agenda when he took office in January 1980. But my advice was totally ignored. The

Reagan team proceeded with its legislative effort to expand IRA availability, and we started to market the 401(k).

I was finally referred to the Treasury official who was drafting regulations for the 401(k) provision. Up to that point, my "invention" was surrounded by uncertainty because the IRS hadn't laid down any guidelines. If the "regs" were negative, they could kill the plan. But if they were supportive, the sky could become the limit in applying the 401(k) concept throughout the country. Finally, the I.R.S. did issue supportive regulations for the 401(k) concept, and that opened the door to a nationwide promotion effort. We had much trouble getting the press to take notice of the 401(k), but Craig Stock of the *Philadelphia Inquirer* finally wrote an article, which was picked up nationally by other newspapers. Stock received literally hundreds of negative calls from human resources executives and attorneys arguing that the idea wasn't legal. That was the same response I got when I went on the stump to promote the idea among prospective clients.

On one trip to see representatives of Prentice Hall, I walked into a conference room expecting a low-key, cordial meeting with two or three members of their staff. Instead, I found myself facing a roomful of rather unfriendly tax experts and writers. It was clear that they wanted to find holes in this new 401(k) idea. But after about an hour of discussion they became quite excited about the concept—and the conversation soon turned to ways that they could get Prentice Hall to adopt such a program. Prentice Hall featured the idea in its executive newsletters in the spring of 1981.

There are now more than 200,000 401(k) savings plans in existence, involving approximately 25 million participants and more than $500 billion in investment capital. And the numbers are growing steadily—with assets in the plans projected to reach $1.25 trillion by the year 2000.

IT'S UP TO *YOU* TO PROTECT YOUR RETIREMENT RIGHTS

I hope my story will drive home the point that it is up to *us*, as individual American citizens, to remain diligent about promoting our retirement rights.

I started the 401(k) Association on August 1, 1993 because I had become increasingly concerned about the future of the 401(k) programs in particular, and about the deterioration of the entire retirement outlook in general. To understand the very real danger that plans like the 401(k) face, it's necessary to view them in the broader context of national politics. Despite the fact that the 401(k) savings plan is now the best investment vehicle available to most workers, no policy maker in Washington has a vested interest in it because he created it. And at the present time, no elected official has come forward as the plan's champion. Furthermore, 401(k)s, like other tax-qualified retirement programs, are a constant drain on tax revenues. The money you invest in tax-sheltered accounts leaves less money for federal coffers.

This type of program—a tax-sheltered retirement plan *without* an official champion—is highly vulnerable to interference by public officials and administrators, who are always looking around for more funds to fuel their projects. The public's only line of defense is to spread the truth about the grassroots benefits of these plans—and also to launch a lobbying effort. That's what we are doing with the 401(k) Association. If you remain passive when plans like the 401(k) come under attack, the likelihood is that there will be no safety net at all to secure your financial future.

WHAT YOU CAN DO

I would suggest this personal strategy to protect those aspects of your retirement that are most important to your financial future.

Step One: Pinpoint the Issues that Concern You Most

Make a list of the retirement funds and systems that will have the greatest impact on you personally. The first choice for nearly everyone should be Social Security.

Next, look at your own retirement package. If you have a defined benefit pension plan, put that on your list. If you have a Keogh, an IRA, or a 401(k), add that. Be sure to include all of your potential sources of retirement income on this list.

Step Two: Write Down the Dangers

Make a list of the greatest dangers that you see threatening the programs on your list. You can get this information from chapter 2 and other relevant sections in this book. You should list each of the areas of concern and the threats that go along with them. You might have one list headed "Social Security Concerns," and the items underneath it might include "increasing taxes on benefits" and "means testing." Or under "IRA Concerns," you might include "restrictions on tax deductibility of contributions."

Step Three: Draw Up a "Movers-and-Shakers" Sheet

List the influential people who may be able to protect your retirement benefits and rights. On the political front, the obvious candidates are your state's members of Congress. In the corporate realm, you might choose the head of the human resources department in your company, or whoever else is in charge of your employer's retirement and pension program. Also, don't forget local community leaders, like the clergy, sympathetic business and charity leaders, and politicians. Anyone who wields any sort of clout can further your cause.

Be sure to write down addresses, proper titles, and telephone and fax numbers. This particular piece of paper should become an "action sheet" for you as you begin to contact these people about your concerns.

Step Four: Be Alert for Opportunities

Watch for an event or "news peg" that will provide you with an opportunity to speak out on retirement issues—and then act!

For example, if you read that Congress is considering restrictions on Social Security, private pensions, or some other issue that affects your retirement, you should immediately pull out your movers-and-shakers sheet and write to the relevant people you have listed. It won't hurt to follow up your letter with a call or fax.

If the issue is going to be resolved in Congress, that doesn't mean you have to limit your advocacy to your local Representative or Senators. You should also consider trying to mobilize the influential local people you have listed in step 3. Ask them to use their influence on the issue. Another effective tactic is to put together a petition relating to your concern. If you can get ten or more people to sign a statement saying that they oppose (or support) certain changes in a retirement program or right, that may go a long way toward influencing an elected representative.

As I've said, at one time I might have believed that one person couldn't make much of a difference. But my experience with the 401(k) movement has convinced me otherwise. In fact, one truly committed person who is willing to stick to an issue like a bulldog can effect major changes in government policy.

Too often, our rights are subverted because we are too passive or complacent. We tend to assume "what will be, will be," and then we go about our business. But retirement and pension trends don't have to continue to go against us—as long as we are willing to speak out.

So if you are really concerned about the direction that retirement is heading in this country, consider doing something about it! It won't take a lot of your time. A timely letter or phone call to your congressional representative or senator can be more important to your secure retirement than you may have realized.

A FINAL PIECE OF ADVICE:
STAY ON TOP OF MARKET NEWS

To protect yourself properly for the future, it's essential for you to stay on top of market news and trends.

In order to stay informed about what's happening in the financial world and thus make proper preparations, let me offer a few guidelines that have worked with many successful individual investors:

Read Several Financial Publications Every Week

At a minimum, you should read thoroughly the daily business section of a paper like *The New York Times*, which provides extensive coverage of business and financial news.

Also, try to read a specialized financial daily like *The Wall Street Journal* every day. Look for stories about companies or funds that you are considering as investments. Follow the price changes of these companies or funds over a period of at least a month before you buy.

In addition, *Investor's Daily*, *Barron's* weekly, *Forbes* magazine, *Money* magazine, and other investor-oriented publications provide a great deal of useful information. You certainly won't understand everything you read in these publications if you're a new investor; various terms, charts, and listings may seem to be written in another language. But stick with it! If you take your time, study these publications, and read some books for the "beginning investor" available in your library or local bookstore, you will quickly get up to speed.

Read Publications that Provide Special Information and Ratings for Mutual Funds

As you know, I'm a great proponent of mutual fund investing because I think it's too hard for the small investor to get the diversity (and safety) he needs by investing in individual stocks on his own. A solid mutual fund, with a good track record over at least the past five years, is definitely the best route for most of us who are not professional investors.

But even if you go the mutual fund route, you will need to understand something about the investment philosophies of the companies you are considering, and also how they have performed in the past. To get this information, you might check the ratings and newsletter put out by Morningstar, Inc., the Chicago funds rating company. Or you may want to buy the annual issue on mutual funds published by either *Kiplingers* or *Forbes* magazine. In addition, *The Wall Street Journal* has been beefing up its mutual fund coverage recently and periodically publishes special sections on mutual funds and related investment topics.

Here is a practical idea that has worked for many investors: Watch a mutual fund that interests you for a month. If you still like it at the end of the month, make a small commitment of money. As you become more comfortable with the investment, add to your fund. By moving slowly, you will give your fears and uncertainties time to subside. There's nothing like experience and knowledge to banish unfounded fears. Then, your confidence will grow even more as you become familiar with the peculiar movements of the investment you have chosen.

Always Look for the Market Opportunities

You should actually look forward to a decrease in the value of your shares. If you are dollar-cost averaging, that decline in price will give you an opportunity to buy additional shares—which will appreciate during the next market upturn and provide you with a nice gain.

By increasing your knowledge of the markets—and becoming more comfortable with what the public often mistakenly perceives as the inordinate risk of common stocks—you will be protecting yourself from the retirement crisis that is well on its way. Self-reliance, not reliance on the government or the promises made by a company, is the only sure route to a comfortable retirement.

Indeed, the safest Americans are those who learn how to save regularly and increase the size of their assets at a reasonable but healthy rate. Such people have taken true responsibility for their own financial future—and they are in a strong position to avoid becoming casualties of the coming retirement crisis.

TABLES

Table A-1
(Earlier in Book as Table 3-6, 4-1, 7-1)
AMOUNT NEEDED TO PROVIDE ONE DOLLAR
OF INFLATION-ADJUSTED INCOME AFTER RETIREMENT

Investment Strategy	*Inflation Rate—3.0%*			
	Number of Years Income Will Be Needed			
	20	25	30	35
Conservative	$16.08	$19.14	$21.90	$24.38
Moderate	13.36	15.29	16.85	18.12
Aggressive	12.16	13.67	14.82	15.71

Investment Strategy	*Inflation Rate—3.5%*			
	Number of Years Income Will Be Needed			
	20	25	30	35
Conservative	$16.78	$20.19	$23.33	$26.23
Moderate	13.91	16.04	17.82	19.30
Aggressive	12.64	14.31	15.62	16.65

Investment Strategy	*Inflation Rate—4.0%*			
	Number of Years Income Will Be Needed			
	20	25	30	35
Conservative	$17.53	$21.32	$24.90	$28.25
Moderate	14.47	16.85	18.88	20.61
Aggressive	13.13	14.99	16.48	17.69

Investment Strategy	*Inflation Rate—4.5%*			
	Number of Years Income Will Be Needed			
	20	25	30	35
Conservative	$18.32	$22.53	$26.60	$30.54
Moderate	15.08	17.72	20.03	22.04
Aggressive	13.66	15.72	17.42	18.82

Investment Strategy	*Inflation Rate—5.0%*			
	Number of Years Income Will Be Needed			
	20	25	30	35
Conservative	$19.16	$23.83	$28.47	$33.05
Moderate	15.71	18.65	21.27	23.62
Aggressive	14.21	16.50	18.43	20.07

Table A-2
(Earlier in Book as Table 3-2, 4-2, 7-2)
INFLATION ADJUSTMENT TABLE

Number of Years	Assumed Annual Rate of Change				
	3%	*3.5%*	*4%*	*4.5%*	*5%*
1	1.03	1.035	1.04	1.045	1.05
2	1.06	1.07	1.08	1.09	1.10
3	1.09	1.11	1.12	1.14	1.16
4	1.12	1.15	1.17	1.19	1.22
5	1.16	1.19	1.22	1.25	1.28
6	1.19	1.23	1.27	1.30	1.34
7	1.23	1.27	1.32	1.36	1.41
8	1.27	1.32	1.37	1.42	1.48
9	1.31	1.36	1.42	1.49	1.55
10	1.34	1.41	1.48	1.55	1.63
11	1.38	1.46	1.54	1.62	1.71
12	1.42	1.51	1.60	1.70	1.80
13	1.46	1.56	1.67	1.77	1.89
14	1.51	1.62	1.73	1.85	1.98
15	1.56	1.68	1.80	1.93	2.08
16	1.60	1.74	1.87	2.02	2.18
17	1.65	1.80	1.95	2.11	2.29
18	1.70	1.86	2.02	2.21	2.41
19	1.75	1.93	2.10	2.31	2.53
20	1.80	1.99	2.19	2.41	2.65
21	1.86	2.06	2.28	2.52	2.79
22	1.91	2.13	2.37	2.63	2.93
23	1.97	2.21	2.46	2.75	3.08
24	2.03	2.29	2.56	2.87	3.23
25	2.09	2.37	2.66	3.00	3.39
26	2.15	2.45	2.77	3.14	3.56
27	2.22	2.53	2.88	3.28	3.74
28	2.28	2.62	3.00	3.43	3.92
29	2.35	2.72	3.12	3.58	4.12
30	2.42	2.81	3.24	3.74	4.33

Table A-3
(Earlier in Book as Table 4-3, 7-3)
TABLE FOR PROJECTING CURRENT SAVINGS BEFORE RETIREMENT

| | **Investment Strategy** | | |
Years	*Conservative*	*Moderate*	*Aggressive*
1	1.062	1.086	1.103
2	1.128	1.179	1.217
3	1.198	1.281	1.342
4	1.272	1.391	1.480
5	1.351	1.511	1.633
6	1.435	1.641	1.801
7	1.524	1.782	1.986
8	1.618	1.935	2.191
9	1.718	2.101	2.416
10	1.825	2.282	2.665
11	1.938	2.478	2.939
12	2.058	2.691	3.242
13	2.186	2.923	3.576
14	2.321	3.174	3.944
15	2.465	3.447	4.351
16	2.618	3.743	4.799
17	2.780	4.065	5.293
18	2.953	4.415	5.839
19	3.136	4.795	6.440
20	3.330	5.207	7.103
21	3.537	5.655	7.835
22	3.756	6.141	8.642
23	3.989	6.669	9.532
24	4.236	7.243	10.514
25	4.499	7.866	11.597
26	4.778	8.542	12.791
27	5.074	9.277	14.109
28	5.389	10.075	15.562
29	5.723	10.941	17.165
30	6.078	11.882	18.933

Table A-4
(Earlier in Book as Table 4-4, 6-2, 7-4)
TABLE FOR PROJECTING ACCUMULATION OF FUTURE RETIREMENT SAVINGS
BEFORE RETIREMENT

	Investment Strategy		
Years	*Conservative*	*Moderate*	*Aggressive*
1	1.000	1.000	1.000
2	2.062	2.086	2.103
3	3.190	3.265	3.320
4	4.388	4.546	4.662
5	5.660	5.937	6.142
6	7.011	7.448	7.774
7	8.445	9.088	9.575
8	9.969	10.870	11.561
9	11.587	12.805	13.752
10	13.305	14.906	16.168
11	15.130	17.188	18.834
12	17.068	19.666	21.774
13	19.126	22.357	25.016
14	21.312	25.280	28.593
15	23.634	28.454	32.538
16	26.099	31.901	36.890
17	28.717	35.645	41.689
18	31.498	39.710	46.983
19	34.450	44.125	52.823
20	37.586	48.920	59.263
21	40.917	54.127	66.367
22	44.454	59.782	74.203
23	48.210	65.923	82.846
24	52.199	72.592	92.379
25	56.435	79.835	102.894
26	60.934	87.701	114.493
27	65.712	96.244	127.285
28	70.786	105.521	141.396
29	76.175	115.595	156.959
30	81.898	126.536	174.126

The above factors are how much $1.00 invested each year will grow to over the applicable number of future years assuming the investment performance for each investment strategy equals historical returns achieved during the period from 1926 through 1993. It has been assumed that the amount you save does not earn any investment income during the year it is invested. This will understate your actual results if you invest the entire amount at the beginning of the year or periodically during the year.

Table A-5
(Earlier in Book as Table 7-5)
DISCOUNTING FROM AGE SIXTY-FIVE TO AN EARLIER RETIREMENT AGE

Number of Years Between Retirement Age and Sixty-Five	Investment Strategy		
	Conservative	*Moderate*	*Aggressive*
1	.942	.921	.907
2	.887	.848	.823
3	.836	.781	.746
4	.787	.719	.677
5	.742	.662	.614
6	.699	.610	.557
7	.658	.561	.505
8	.620	.517	.458
9	.584	.476	.415
10	.550	.438	.376
11	.518	.404	.341
12	.488	.372	.310
13	.460	.342	.281
14	.433	.315	.255
15	.408	.290	.231

Table A-6
FOR PROJECTING CURRENT RETIREMENT ACCOUNT

Years	Conservative	Investment Strategy Moderate	Aggressive
1	1.074	1.086	1.103
2	1.153	1.179	1.217
3	1.239	1.281	1.342
4	1.331	1.391	1.480
5	1.429	1.511	1.633
6	1.535	1.641	1.801
7	1.649	1.782	1.987
8	1.771	1.935	2.191
9	1.902	2.101	2.417
10	2.043	2.282	2.666
11	2.194	2.478	2.941
12	2.356	2.691	3.244
13	2.530	2.923	3.578
14	2.718	3.174	3.946
15	2.919	3.447	4.353
16	3.135	3.473	4.801
17	3.367	4.065	5.296
18	3.616	4.415	5.841
19	3.884	4.795	6.443
20	4.171	5.207	7.107
21	4.480	5.655	7.839
22	4.811	6.141	8.646
23	5.167	6.669	9.537
24	5.550	7.243	10.519
25	5.960	7.866	11.602
26	6.401	8.542	12.797
27	6.875	9.277	14.115
28	7.384	10.075	15.569
29	7.930	10.941	17.173
30	8.517	11.882	18.942

The above factors are how much $1.00 will grow to over the applicable number of future years assuming that the investment performance for each investment strategy equals historical returns achieved during the period from 1926 through 1993.

Table A-7
$50,000 EMERGENCY NEST EGG GROWN OVER TWENTY YEARS

Number of Years	$50,000* "Real" Nest Egg	Amount Needed Investment Strategy		
		Conservative	Moderate	Aggressive
Initial Sum ▷ 50,000		**36,095**	**23,861**	**19,106**
1	51,750	37,972	25,627	20,749
2	53,561	39,947	27,523	22,533
3	55,436	42,024	29,560	24,471
4	57,376	44,209	31,747	26,576
5	59,384	46,508	34,096	28,862
6	61,462	48,927	36,620	31,344
7	63,613	51,471	39,329	34,040
8	65,839	54,147	42,239	36,967
9	68,143	56,963	45,365	40,147
10	70,528	59,925	48,722	43,599
11	72,996	63,041	52,327	47,349
12	75,551	66,319	56,199	51,421
13	78,195	69,768	60,358	55,843
14	80,932	73,396	64,824	60,646
15	83,765	77,213	69,622	65,862
16	86,697	81,228	74,774	71,523
17	89,731	85,452	80,307	77,674
18	92,872	89,895	86,250	84,354
19	96,123	94,569	92,632	91,609
20	99,487	99,487	99,487	99,487

Adjusted for inflation at 3.5% rate.

Table A-8
(Earlier in Book as Table 3-7)
$50,000 EMERGENCY NEST EGG GROWN OVER TWENTY-FIVE YEARS

		Amount Needed		
Number of Years	$50,000* "Real" Nest Egg	Investment Strategy		
		Conservative	Moderate	Aggressive
Initial Sum◊	50,000	*33,272*	*19,832*	*15,022*
1	51,750	35,002	21,300	16,314
2	53,561	36,822	22,876	17,717
3	55,436	38,737	24,569	19,241
4	57,376	40,751	26,387	20,895
5	59,384	42,870	28,340	22,692
6	61,462	45,099	30,437	24,644
7	63,613	47,445	32,689	26,763
8	65,839	49,912	35,108	29,065
9	68,143	52,507	37,706	31,564
10	70,528	55,238	40,496	34,279
11	72,996	58,110	43,493	37,227
12	75,551	61,132	46,711	40,428
13	78,195	64,310	50,168	43,905
14	80,932	67,655	53,880	47,681
15	83,765	71,173	57,868	51,781
16	86,697	74,874	62,150	56,235
17	89,731	78,767	66,749	61,071
18	92,872	82,863	71,688	66,323
19	96,123	87,172	76,993	72,027
20	99,487	91,705	82,691	78,221
21	102,969	96,473	88,810	84,948
22	106,573	101,490	95,382	92,253
23	110,303	106,767	102,440	100,187
24	114,164	112,319	110,020	108,803
25	118,160	118,160	118,162	118,160

*Adjusted for inflation at 3.5% rate.

Table A-9
$50,000 EMERGENCY NEST EGG GROWN OVER THIRTY YEARS

Number of Years	$50,000* "Real" Nest Egg	Amount Needed		
		Investment Strategy		
		Conservative	Moderate	Aggressive
Initial Sum◊ 50,000		**30,699**	**16,483**	**11,811**
1	51,750	32,264	17,703	12,827
2	53,561	33,941	19,013	13,930
3	55,436	35,706	20,420	15,128
4	57,376	37,563	21,931	16,429
5	59,384	39,516	23,554	17,842
6	61,462	41,571	25,297	19,376
7	63,613	43,733	27,169	21,042
8	65,839	46,007	29,179	22,852
9	68,143	48,399	31,338	24,817
10	70,528	50,916	33,657	26,952
11	72,996	53,564	36,148	29,269
12	75,551	56,349	38,823	31,787
13	78,195	59,279	41,696	34,520
14	80,932	62,362	44,781	37,489
15	83,765	65,605	48,095	40,713
16	86,697	69,016	51,654	44,214
17	89,731	72,605	55,476	48,017
18	92,872	76,380	59,582	52,146
19	96,123	80,352	63,991	56,631
20	99,487	84,530	68,726	61,501
21	102,969	88,926	73,812	66,790
22	106,573	93,550	79,274	72,534
23	110,303	98,415	85,140	78,772
24	114,164	103,532	91,440	85,546
25	118,160	108,916	98,207	92,903
26	122,296	114,580	105,474	100,893
27	126,576	120,538	113,279	109,570
28	131,006	126,806	121,662	118,993
29	135,591	133,400	130,665	129,226
30	140,337	140,336	140,334	140,339

Adjusted for inflation at 3.5% rate.

Table A-10
MANAGING YOUR NEST EGG OVER TWENTY YEARS
Conservative Investment Strategy After Retirement—5.2% Return

Number of Years	Beginning of Year Balance	Annual* Withdrawal	Investment Return	End of Year Balance
1	167,828	(10,000)	8,467	166,295
2	166,295	(10,350)	8,378	164,323
3	164,323	(10,712)	8,266	161,877
4	161,877	(11,087)	8,129	158,919
5	158,919	(11,475)	7,965	155,408
6	155,408	(11,877)	7,772	151,303
7	151,303	(12,293)	7,548	146,559
8	146,559	(12,723)	7,290	141,126
9	141,126	(13,168)	6,996	134,954
10	134,954	(13,629)	6,663	127,988
11	127,988	(14,106)	6,289	120,171
12	120,171	(14,600)	5,869	111,440
13	111,440	(15,111)	5,402	101,732
14	101,732	(15,640)	4,883	90,975
15	90,975	(16,187)	4,310	79,098
16	79,098	(16,753)	3,678	66,023
17	66,023	(17,340)	2,982	51,665
18	51,665	(17,947)	2,220	35,938
19	35,938	(18,575)	1,386	18,749
20	18,749	(19,225)	475	(1)
TOTALS		(282,797)	114,968	

*Equal to $10,000 adjusted annually for inflation assuming a 3.5%·inflation rate.
It has been assumed the withdrawal will take place at the middle of the year.*

Table A-11
(Earlier in Book as Table 3-3)

MANAGING YOUR NEST EGG OVER TWENTY-FIVE YEARS
Conservative Investment Strategy After Retirement—5.2% Return

Number of Years	Beginning of Year Balance	Annual* Withdrawal	Investment Return	End of Year Balance
1	201,910	(10,000)	10,239	202,149
2	202,149	(10,350)	10,243	202,042
3	202,042	(10,712)	10,228	201,558
4	201,558	(11,087)	10,193	200,664
5	200,664	(11,475)	10,136	199,324
6	199,324	(11,877)	10,056	197,503
7	197,503	(12,293)	9,951	195,162
8	195,162	(12,723)	9,818	192,257
9	192,257	(13,168)	9,655	188,744
10	188,744	(13,629)	9,460	184,575
11	184,575	(14,106)	9,231	179,700
12	179,700	(14,600)	8,965	174,065
13	174,065	(15,111)	8,659	167,614
14	167,614	(15,640)	8,309	160,283
15	160,283	(16,187)	7,914	152,010
16	152,010	(16,753)	7,469	142,726
17	142,726	(17,340)	6,971	132,357
18	132,357	(17,947)	6,416	120,826
19	120,826	(18,575)	5,800	108,051
20	108,051	(19,225)	5,119	93,945
21	93,945	(19,898)	4,368	78,415
22	78,415	(20,594)	3,542	61,363
23	61,363	(21,315)	2,637	42,685
24	42,685	(22,061)	1,646	22,270
25	22,270	(22,833)	564	0
TOTALS		(389,499)	187,589	

Equal to $10,000 adjusted annually for inflation assuming a 3.5% inflation rate. It has been assumed the withdrawal will take place at the middle of the year.

Table A-12
MANAGING YOUR NEST EGG OVER THIRTY YEARS
Conservative Investment Strategy After Retirement—5.2% Return

Number of Years	Beginning of Year Balance	Annual* Withdrawal	Investment Return	End of Year Balance
1	233,330	(10,000)	11,873	235,203
2	235,203	(10,350)	11,961	236,814
3	236,814	(10,712)	12,036	238,138
4	238,138	(11,087)	12,095	239,146
5	239,146	(11,475)	12,137	239,807
6	239,807	(11,877)	12,161	240,091
7	240,091	(12,293)	12,165	239,964
8	239,964	(12,723)	12,147	239,388
9	239,388	(13,168)	12,106	238,326
10	238,326	(13,629)	12,039	236,736
11	236,736	(14,106)	11,944	234,574
12	234,574	(14,600)	11,818	231,792
13	231,792	(15,111)	11,660	228,342
14	228,342	(15,640)	11,467	224,169
15	224,169	(16,187)	11,236	219,218
16	219,218	(16,753)	10,964	213,429
17	213,429	(17,340)	10,647	206,736
18	206,736	(17,947)	10,284	199,073
19	199,073	(18,575)	9,869	190,367
20	190,367	(19,225)	9,399	180,541
21	180,541	(19,898)	8,871	169,514
22	169,514	(20,594)	8,279	157,199
23	157,199	(21,315)	7,620	143,504
24	143,504	(22,061)	6,889	128,33
25	128,332	(22,833)	6,080	111,578
26	111,578	(23,632)	5,188	93,134
27	93,134	(24,460)	4,207	72,881
28	72,881	(25,316)	3,132	50,698
29	50,698	(26,202)	1,955	26,451
30	26,451	(27,119)	670	2
TOTALS		(516,227)	282,899	

Equal to $10,000 adjusted annually for inflation assuming a 3.5% inflation rate. It has been assumed the withdrawal will take place at the middle of the year.

Table A-13
MANAGING YOUR NEST EGG OVER TWENTY YEARS
Moderate Investment Strategy After Retirement—7.4% Return

Number of Years	Beginning of Year Balance	Annual* Withdrawal	Investment Return	End of Year Balance
1	139,005	(10,000)	9,916	138,921
2	138,921	(10,350)	9,897	138,468
3	138,468	(10,712)	9,850	137,606
4	137,606	(11,087)	9,773	136,292
5	136,292	(11,475)	9,661	134,478
6	134,478	(11,877)	9,512	132,113
7	132,113	(12,293)	9,321	129,141
8	129,141	(12,723)	9,086	125,504
9	125,504	(13,168)	8,800	121,136
10	121,136	(13,629)	8,460	115,967
11	115,967	(14,106)	8,060	109,921
12	109,921	(14,600)	7,594	102,915
13	102,915	(15,111)	7,057	94,861
14	94,861	(15,640)	6,441	85,662
15	85,662	(16,187)	5,740	75,215
16	75,215	(16,753)	4,946	63,408
17	63,408	(17,340)	4,051	50,119
18	50,119	(17,947)	3,045	35,217
19	35,217	(18,575)	1,919	18,561
20	18,561	(19,225)	662	(2)
TOTALS		(282,798)	143,791	

Equal to $10,000 adjusted annually for inflation assuming a 3.5% inflation rate. It has been assumed the withdrawal will take place at the middle of the year.

Table A-14
(Earlier in Book as Table 3-4)
MANAGING YOUR NEST EGG OVER TWENTY-FIVE YEARS
Moderate Investment Strategy After Retirement—7.4% Return

Number of Years	Beginning of Year Balance	Annual* Withdrawal	Investment Return	End of Year Balance
1	160,430	(10,000)	11,502	161,932
2	161,932	(10,350)	11,600	163,182
3	163,182	(10,712)	11,679	164,149
4	164,149	(11,087)	11,737	164,799
5	164,799	(11,475)	11,771	165,099
6	165,094	(11,877)	11,778	164,996
7	164,995	(12,293)	11,755	164,458
8	164,458	(12,723)	11,699	163,434
9	163,434	(13,168)	11,607	161,873
10	161,873	(13,629)	11,474	159,718
11	159,718	(14,106)	11,297	156,909
12	156,909	(14,600)	11,071	153,380
13	153,380	(15,111)	10,791	149,060
14	149,060	(15,640)	10,452	143,872
15	143,872	(16,187)	10,048	137,733
16	137,733	(16,753)	9,572	130,552
17	130,552	(17,340)	9,019	122,231
18	122,231	(17,947)	8,381	112,665
19	112,665	(18,575)	7,650	101,740
20	101,740	(19,225)	6,818	89,333
21	89,333	(19,898)	5,875	75,310
22	75,310	(20,594)	4,811	59,527
23	59,527	(21,315)	3,616	41,828
24	41,828	(22,061)	2,279	22,046
25	22,046	(22,833)	787	0
TOTALS		(389,499)	229,069	

Equal to $10,000 adjusted annually for inflation assuming a 3.5% inflation rate. It has been asumed the withdrawal will take place at the middle of the year.

Table A-15
MANAGING YOUR NEST EGG OVER THIRTY YEARS
Moderate Investment Strategy After Retirement—7.4% Return

Number of Years	Beginning of Year Balance	Annual* Withdrawal	Investment Return	End of Year Balance
1	178,240	(10,000)	12,820	181,060
2	181,060	(10,350)	13,015	183,725
3	183,725	(10,712)	13,199	186,212
4	186,212	(11,087)	13,369	188,494
5	188,494	(11,475)	13,524	190,543
6	190,543	(11,877)	13,661	192,327
7	192,327	(12,293)	13,777	193,811
8	193,811	(12,723)	13,871	194,959
9	194,959	(13,168)	13,940	195,731
10	195,731	(13,629)	13,980	196,082
11	196,082	(14,106)	13,988	195,964
12	195,964	(14,600)	13,961	195,325
13	195,325	(15,111)	13,895	194,109
14	194,109	(15,640)	13,785	192,254
15	192,254	(16,187)	13,628	189,695
16	189,695	(16,753)	13,418	186,360
17	186,360	(17,340)	13,149	182,169
18	182,169	(17,947)	12,817	177,039
19	177,039	(18,575)	12,414	170,878
20	170,878	(19,225)	11,934	163,587
21	163,587	(19,898)	11,369	155,058
22	155,058	(20,594)	10,712	145,176
23	145,176	(21,315)	9,954	133,815
24	133,815	(22,061)	9,086	120,840
25	120,840	(22,833)	8,097	106,104
26	106,104	(23,632)	6,977	89,449
27	89,449	(24,460)	5,714	70,703
28	70,703	(25,316)	4,295	49,682
29	49,682	(26,202)	2,707	26,187
30	26,187	(27,119)	935	3
TOTALS		(516,227)	337,991	

Equal to $10,000 adjusted annually for inflation assuming a 3.5% inflation rate. It has been assumed the withdrawal will take place at the middle of the year.

Table A-16
MANAGING YOUR NEST EGG OVER TWENTY YEARS
Aggressive Investment Strategy After Retirement—8.6% Return

Number of Years	Beginning of Year Balance	Annual* Withdrawal	Investment Return	End of Year Balance
1	126,361	(10,000)	10,437	126,798
2	126,798	(10,350)	10,460	126,908
3	126,908	(10,712)	10,453	126,649
4	126,649	(11,087)	10,415	125,977
5	125,977	(11,475)	10,341	124,843
6	124,843	(11,877)	10,226	123,192
7	123,192	(12,293)	10,066	120,965
8	120,965	(12,723)	9,856	118,098
9	118,098	(13,168)	9,590	114,520
10	114,520	(13,629)	9,263	110,154
11	110,154	(14,106)	8,867	104,915
12	104,915	(14,600)	8,395	98,710
13	98,710	(15,111)	7,839	91,438
14	91,438	(15,640)	7,191	82,989
15	82,989	(16,187)	6,441	73,243
16	73,243	(16,753)	5,579	62,069
17	62,069	(17,340)	4,592	49,321
18	49,321	(17,947)	3,470	34,844
19	34,844	(18,575)	2,198	18,467
20	18,467	(19,225)	762	4
TOTALS		(282,797)	156,441	

Equal to $10,000 adjusted annually for inflation assuming a 3.5% inflation rate. It has been assumed the withdrawal will take place at the middle of the year.

Table A-17
(Earlier in Book as Table 3-5)
MANAGING YOUR NEST EGG OVER TWENTY-FIVE YEARS
Aggressive Investment Strategy After Retirement—8.6% Return

Number of Years	Beginning of Year Balance	Annual* Withdrawal	Investment Return	End of Year Balance
1	143,065	(10,000)	11,874	144,939
2	144,939	(10,350)	12,020	146,609
3	146,609	(10,712)	12,148	148,045
4	148,045	(11,087)	12,255	149,213
5	149,213	(11,475)	12,339	150,077
6	150,077	(11,877)	12,396	150,596
7	150,596	(12,293)	12,423	150,726
8	150,726	(12,723)	12,415	150,418
9	150,418	(13,168)	12,370	149,620
10	149,620	(13,629)	12,281	148,272
11	148,272	(14,106)	12,145	146,311
12	146,311	(14,600)	11,955	143,666
13	143,666	(15,111)	11,706	140,261
14	140,261	(15,640)	11,390	136,011
15	136,011	(16,187)	11,001	130,826
16	130,826	(16,753)	10,531	124,604
17	124,604	(17,340)	9,970	117,234
18	117,234	(17,947)	9,310	108,597
19	108,597	(18,575)	8,541	98,563
20	98,563	(19,225)	7,650	86,988
21	86,988	(19,898)	6,625	73,715
22	73,715	(20,594)	5,454	58,575
23	58,575	(21,315)	4,121	41,381
24	41,381	(22,061)	2,610	21,930
25	21,930	(22,833)	904	1
TOTALS		(389,499)	246,434	

Equal to $10,000 adjusted annually for inflation assuming a 3.5% inflation rate. It has been assumed the withdrawal will take place at the middle of the year.

Table A-18
MANAGING YOUR NEST EGG OVER THIRTY YEARS
Aggressive Investment Strategy After Retirement—8.6% Return

Number of Years	Beginning of Year Balance	Annual* Withdrawal	Investment Return	End of Year Balance
1	156,201	(10,000)	13,003	159,204
2	159,204	(10,350)	13,246	162,100
3	162,100	(10,712)	13,480	164,868
4	164,868	(11,087)	13,702	167,483
5	167,483	(11,475)	13,910	169,918
6	169,918	(11,877)	14,102	172,143
7	172,143	(12,293)	14,276	174,126
8	174,126	(12,723)	14,428	175,831
9	175,831	(13,168)	14,555	177,218
10	177,218	(13,629)	14,655	178,244
11	178,244	(14,106)	14,722	178,860
12	178,860	(14,600)	14,754	179,014
13	179,014	(15,111)	14,745	178,648
14	178,648	(15,640)	14,691	177,699
15	177,699	(16,187)	14,586	176,098
16	176,098	(16,753)	14,424	173,769
17	173,769	(17,340)	14,199	170,628
18	170,628	(17,947)	13,902	166,583
19	166,583	(18,575)	13,528	161,536
20	161,536	(19,225)	13,066	155,377
21	155,377	(19,898)	12,507	147,987
22	147,987	(20,594)	11,841	139,234
23	139,234	(21,315)	11,058	128,977
24	128,977	(22,061)	10,143	117,059
25	117,059	(22,833)	9,085	103,311
26	103,311	(23,632)	7,869	87,548
27	87,548	(24,460)	6,477	69,565
28	69,565	(25,316)	4,894	49,143
29	49,143	(26,202)	3,100	26,041
30	26,041	(27,119)	1,073	(5)
TOTALS		(516,228)	360,021	

Equal to $10,000 adjusted annually for inflation assuming a 3.5% inflation rate. It has been assumed the withdrawal will take place at the middle of the year.

Table A-19
WHAT YOU CAN EXPECT TODAY IN SOCIAL SECURITY BENEFITS

The following table shows benefits payable to the worker and spouse. To use the table, find the age that is closest to your current age and the earnings closest to your earnings in the previous year. These figures will give you an estimate of the amount of your retirement benefits at various ages.

APPROXIMATE MONTHLY RETIREMENT BENEFITS IF THE WORKER RETIRES AT NORMAL RETIREMENT AGE AND HAD STEADY LIFETIME EARNINGS

Worker's Current Age	Worker's Family	Retired Worker's Earnings in Previous Year					
		$10,000	$20,000	$30,000	$40,000	$50,000	Maximum Wage Base or More[1]
25	Retired worker only	$ 519	$ 780	$ 1,047	$ 1,183	$ 1,308	$ 1,448
	Worker and spouse[2]	778	1,170	1,570	1,774	1,962	2,172
	Replacement rate[3]	62%	47%	42%	35%	31%	29%
35	Retired worker only	519	779	1,045	1,182	1,307	1,445
	Worker and spouse[2]	778	1,168	1,567	1,774	1,960	2,167
	Replacement rate[3]	62%	47%	42%	35%	31%	29%
45	Retired worker only	519	775	1,039	1,178	1,302	1,418
	Worker and spouse[2]	778	1,162	1,558	1,767	1,953	2,127
	Replacement rate[3]	62%	46%	42%	35%	31%	28%
55	Retired worker only	519	770	1,033	1,163	1,253	1,325
	Worker and spouse[2]	778	1,155	1,549	1,744	1,879	1,987
	Replacement rate[3]	62%	46%	41%	35%	30%	26%
65	Retired worker only	519	761	1,014	1,111	1,166	1,199
	Worker and spouse[2]	778	1,141	1,521	1,666	1,749	1,798
	Replacement rate[3]	62%	45%	41%	33%	28%	24%

1. Earnings equal to, or greater than, the OASDI wage base from age twenty-two through the year before retirement.
2. Spouse is assumed to be the same age as the worker. Spouse may qualify for a higher retirement benefit based on his or her own work record.
3. Replacement rates are shown for retired worker only.

Note: The accuracy of these estimates depends on the pattern of the worker's actual past earnings, and on his or her earnings in the future. Estimates for future retirees are calculated on the same basis used for the Personal Earnings and Benefit Estimate Statement (PEBES).

Table A-20
EXAMPLES OF REDUCED BENEFITS AT EARLY RETIREMENT

If You Retire at Age	You Will Receive This Percent of Your PIA1	Or the Following Benefit If Your PIA1 Is		
		$400	$600	$800
65	100	$400	$600	$800
64 ½	96 ⅔	386	580	773
64	93 ⅓	373	560	746
63 ½	90	360	540	720
63	86 ⅔	346	520	693
62 ½	83 ⅓	333	500	666
62	80	320	480	640

1. Primary insurance amount. You may retire at any time between the ages shown. The reduction is ⅝ of 1 percent for each month that you receive your benefit before age sixty-five.
These reduction factors are for workers only. Different reduction factors are used for spouses.

My Financial Notes

MY FINANCIAL NOTES

My Financial Notes

My Financial Notes

My Financial Notes

MY FINANCIAL NOTES

MY FINANCIAL NOTES

MY FINANCIAL NOTES

My Financial Notes

MY FINANCIAL NOTES